GEN-X the ADULT ERA

Designing a
Life of
Wellness

(On Our Own, As Usual)

APRIL RAQUE
NBC-HWC

Cover design by Nancy Iannitelli and Rebeca Seitz

Printed in the United States of America
Published in the United States of America

Rebeca Books
The 1C Story Network
933 Creech Rd #8
Naples, FL 34103
Rebecabooks.com

Rebeca Books is the publishing division of The 1C Story Network.

The publisher is not responsible for websites (or their content) that are not owned by the publisher.

The 1C Speakers Bureau provides a wide range of content creators, experts, authors, and more for speaking events. To find out more, visit justonec.com or call (407) 490-2690.

Library of Congress Control Number: 2025942856

Tradepaper ISBN 978-0-9970642-4-7

9 8 7 6 5 4 3 2 1
1st edition, October 2025

to my husband for always lifting me up,
even with all my midlife sass...
to my mother for being a good sport
and sharing her journey with me...
to my sisters for their unwavering love...
to my father for being my rock to stand on...
and to God for giving me strength, direction,
and the words to share.

The Deets

/dēts/
noun

1. details.
Ex. "Stay tuned for more deets."

(contents)

Props

/präps/
noun

1. respect or credit due to a person.
Ex. *"This book is already getting props from its friends."*

(advance praise)

Thank you for speaking my language. I need more of you in my life, April.
- Anne Shadle, Co-owner of Mayan Café / Founder of Left Brain Solutions
Consulting

Gen-X, the Adult Era is a bold, honest and heartfelt invitation to age with
intention, authenticity, and power, allowing women to redefine midlife on
their own terms. April brings humor, wisdom, and lived experience to topics
such as menopause, self-care, aging, and mindfulness, which cuts through the
confusion of this modern era with clarity and grace. April shares her personal
journey with remarkable vulnerability and insight, offering a new way to
experience midlife by prioritizing wellness, harmony, and self-defined beauty.
Blending American cultural touchpoints from the Gen-X era with actionable
steps for wellbeing and fulfillment, this book is not a guide but a permission
slip to release old narratives and live more fully and confidently as YOU!
- Dr. KTap, Physician, Wellness Leadership Coach, Speaker, and Owner of
GLOW Coaching

A must-read for women looking to laugh and get real tips with actionable
advice on managing health and life in our 40+ years. I wish I had read it at 30.
- Tiffany Wright, Menopause Thriver, Lady in Tech, and Co-host of the popular
podcast, *Gov Tech Talks*
Gen-X, the Adult Era rings so very true and is so very relatable. As a Gen-X(er),
I found myself reliving and laughing at April Raque's personal experiences,
finding it totally CRAZY how she described my youth and young adult traumas
and triumphs as if she were there! We would've TOTALLY been friends had we
known one another! She reminded me of how rich, carefree, and adventurous
life was back in the day and that we were resourceful, resilient, and fearless!
I miss those days, and this book put my feelings into words and let me revisit

them. I would recommend this book to all Gen-X(ers) or any other generation that wants to know how it really went down.
- Helen Peabody, RN

April Raque's *Gen-X, the Adult Era: Designing A Life of Wellness* is the How-To of WTF for Gen-X women. Her mix tape of actionable advice blends wisdom, wisecracks, and woowoo together to create the how to guide we never got, and desperately need for Menopause and beyond. - Lisa Schmahl, Yoga teacher, Mama, and Mentor

Gen-X, the Adult Era: Designing a Life of Wellness is a beautiful, soul-stirring guide for anyone navigating midlife and looking to reconnect with their most authentic self. Through heartfelt stories, practical tools, and powerful reflections, this book inspires us to shift our mindset, embrace change, and reclaim our personal power. From mindfulness and positivity to managing stress and finding harmony during life's transitions—including menopause—each chapter feels like a supportive conversation with a wise friend. It reminds us that we're not alone in our struggles, and we all have the ability to reframe, rise, and redesign a life that truly feels aligned. A must-read for anyone ready to step into their next chapter with intention and self-love.
- Melissa Severance, PCC, Owner of Inspire Big Dreams

When I hit menopause at 45, my friend April was there for me in a way nobody else could be. We laughed and shared our challenges, and somehow talking it through with April made it all feel less overwhelming. Now she's done the same for every other Gen-X woman with this book. It's honest, funny, practical, and full of the kind of real talk we all need but rarely get. And because April's also a deeply knowledgeable wellness coach with serious training and expertise, it's like having your smartest, sassiest girlfriend in your corner, who also happens to know the research-backed science and exactly how to help. I highly recommend this book to all women going through "The Change." It's high time we all start talking about it, and I can think of no better book than this one to guide you on your journey.
- Susan Baroncini-Moe, CEO, Baroncini-Moe Executive Coaching

Your Mom

/yôr,ÿoor/ /maːm/
interjection

1. a general-purpose insult, often used to comedic
effect due to becoming stale.
Ex. "What's for dinner? Your mom!"

(intro)

If you've heard one "Your Mom" joke, you've heard them all. I
probably said three of them already today. It's become even more
of a staple in my house when talking to my kiddo about almost
everything. Now that he's out of the house, I have menopause to keep
the jokes alive. These days, I'll do anything for a laugh as opposed to
crying about all of the crazy that is midlife.

I'm not blaming my mom. She did her best, but it sure as hell
would have been a lot easier if she would have shared more about
her life experiences–specifically menopause experiences—to help me
prepare for my turn at bat. Unfortunately, I wasn't prepared. Come to
find out, neither are most of the other 30 million Gen-X women. Over
the past few years, I've begun to have more and more conversations
with my sisters, friends, clients, and even my mom about being a
woman, navigating the midlife journey, and how we can age better.

Hell, we barely got to be kids in the '70s and '80s. Dare I say,
thrown to the wolves? We had to figure it all out for ourselves, no

guidance, just a key to the house and a phone number for emergencies, then we were shoved out the door to school.

However, being raised as a Gen-X kid did have its advantages. We learned to overcome obstacles without adult input or oversight and had to find ways to meet our own needs with whatever we could find in the kitchen. We were shaped into great mid-level managers by the responsibility of watching our siblings or babysitting children down the street, and we learned to be resilient and unwavering in our commitments by picking ourselves up and dusting ourselves off.

Is it any wonder we're all left to figure out midlife as well? If you're like me, you're frustrated, exhausted, and too independent to ask for help. You're ready to do the work, but have no idea where to start. You're not taking this transition to Golden Girl lightly. However, you struggle with being seen and taken seriously. Worthiness issues, Imposter Syndrome, fear of failure, shame, and guilt are all present. Have I missed anything here?

Just for kicks, I recently read the description of a female midlife crisis. Lo and behold, the symptoms they described are exactly the same as the symptoms of perimenopause. Who knew? The depression, anxiety, irritability, mood swings, sleep disturbances, weight gain or loss, and increased indecisiveness are only the beginning of a long line of reasons we're all collectively losing it.

We're in constant survival mode and have been since childhood, so it's no wonder we're all looking for a way out, a way to have it better, a way to redefine midlife and aging that takes our nervous system down a notch and allows us to be, just for a moment, real about it.

Gone are the days when terms like "middle-aged," "old hag," "has-been," "over the hill," and "dried up" are used to describe a woman in her fifties. More and more of us are throwing out the old stigmas and changing the way we age. We aren't sitting in our rocking chairs letting the aging process take us alive. We're embracing life, our wrinkles, and our menopause journey and deciding to have it differently. Our generation is single-handedly redefining what it means to be 50. We're breaking this age-old stigma because we're finally using our voices to scream our best "We're Not Gonna Take It" like Twisted Sister. Now let's do this nice and loud ladies, "We're not gonna take it. No! We ain't gonna take it. We're not gonna take it anymore!"[1]

This active aging situation is part of the collective change that happens when you start talking about midlife expectation, what aging isn't, what happens during the menopause transition, and deciding you're not going to take it lying down. Gen-X was built to break barriers and say to hell with preset expectations. We were made for this because we've experienced life to its fullest extent, survived all it handed us, and now we are ready to embrace this change and shift what it means to be a middle-age woman. After all, Gen-X women pride ourselves on our take-no-shit, give-no-shits, and fuck-the-establishment battle cry. We are stronger not in spite of but *because of* all the criticism, undermining, and underestimation we've endured.

Well, life begins at fifty, and we *can* prove it. I mean, you can't get more punk rock or Gen-X than navigating perimenopause during a worldwide pandemic and coming out the other side with everyone in the house still alive—a true miracle. Now is the time we get to learn more about ourselves, know our worth, embrace our authenticity, let our dynamic energy flow, celebrate our imperfections, and see our inner beauty shine as we rally together and make change.

I am writing this book as not only a battle cry, but in hopes that you gain a better understanding of what aging and midlife are and are not. This is your complete guide to redefining your very existence, taking back your power, determining fact from fiction, being fulfilled, feeling vibrant, and navigating all the nuances of life in order to have the beautiful life you deserve. This journey is not for the faint of heart, which is ideal for the Gen-X woman who is not giving up on having the life she deserves. Embarking on my own personal journey toward the life I longed to live is how every chapter of this book was actualized. I am still on my journey and continue to learn and grow into my own. So trust me when I say it is a marathon, not a sprint, but it is worth the sweat. These are my secrets to aging well.
I'm prepared to share all my stories in all their gory details. Within these pages, you'll learn what I've learned throughout my health and wellness training. This guide is here to help you navigate those difficult moments and leave you with a few actionable steps to move along on your journey, designing the life of wellness you deserve.
I'm spilling my guts the only way I know how ("...that's just a little bit more than the law will allow,"[2] *Dukes of Hazzard* style) and in a

way only a Gen-X woman can comprehend. If it's cool with you, I'll be referencing our slang, movies, music, and Gen-X history to keep it all real.

I can't wait to get this party started, so let's dive in.

Lame

/lām/
adjective

2. something intended to be entertaining, but instead is
uninspiring and dull.
Ex. *"I found the lecture on menopause pretty lame and not very
informative."*

(mid-life and the menopausal madness)

FIRE!!!!

I am soaked and freaking hot. Seriously, I'm dripping like I just
came out of the ocean. I roll over to tap my phone, and it's four in the
morning. I can't even see my way around the room, but I have got to
get out of these blankets and sheets, take all my clothes off as quickly
as humanly possible, and slake this insane thirst. I need to get all the
towels laid over my side of the bed so I can finally lie down, breathe,
and let it pass.

We call this: HOT FLASH!

Why did nobody warn me about the perils of midlife and
menopause? I thought midlife meant we all got sports cars and
divorced. Oh yeah, and when did it become perimenopause and
menopause and now post-menopause? Exhausting at best, midlife
and menopause (in any or all the phases) are completely and utterly
LAME. With 34 known symptoms and not nearly enough research,

we're supposed to navigate these hormonal raging rapids in a canoe with no paddle.

Fact: Menopause (in all its states) is inevitable for women. To quote the great *Facts of Life*, "You take the good, you take the bad, you take them both, and there you have, the facts of life."[3] Though I've used this quote many times throughout my life, it seems to ring most true when associated with menopause.

While there are several menopausal symptoms, there are a few worth mentioning by name. During perimenopause and even sometimes after, most women will experience mood swings, decreased sex drive, headaches, fatigue, weight gain (especially in the belly), insomnia, incontinence, and the dreaded hot flashes. Lucky me, I've experienced all of the above in all their glory.

I remember waking up in the middle of the night and just being drenched in sweat. You know, the kind of drenched that has you reaching for a towel and stripping off all your clothes, only to find that you immediately have the chills—but can't jump back in bed because everything is soaked.

Along with the sweat came an urgent need to pee. I ran to the bathroom, naked, stumbling over my dog, launching myself off a pile of my husband's clothes, and slipping on the rug all before finally reaching the dark bathroom and peeing on the seat as I tried to sit down.

Not my best moment.

To make matters even better, once I got cleaned up, dried off, and back to bed, I couldn't get back to sleep for anything. It was like living in the worst sitcom ever. The bitch of it was that this was only the beginning. I proceeded to wake up every night, multiple times, and have the exact same experience for several weeks before I finally realized it wasn't going away. I didn't even associate it with menopause, because, quite frankly, I was too young for that—wasn't I?

My first stop was the gynecologist. I asked her if I was in menopause; and she assured me that I was too young for that and then, after a quick blood test, advised that it was unlikely and politely dismissed my concerns. I was 45 years old at the time, and my symptoms were a valid concern—just not to my doctor. She never asked me a thing about my lifestyle, stress levels, what I ate, if I exercised, or anything about me in order to determine why this nightly bad sitcom scene kept happening. She did tell me to lose weight, but this had become somewhat of an inside joke I feel we all share with our physicians, which I quickly forgot.

So, what was a midlife Gen-X-er to do?

I looked to the East.

I am a long-time proponent of Eastern medicine and have used acupuncture, Chinese medicine, homeopathy, and herbal remedies for insomnia, colds, sore muscles, digestion issues, and other medical situations throughout my life. Why should this situation be any different? With my Western medicine doctor failing me, I did the only thing I knew how to do and called my Chinese medical practitioner to make an appointment for acupuncture.

When I got to the office, I shared my story of woe. To my surprise, the doctor wasn't really that impressed. He checked my *chi*, put a few needles in very tender spots, and got busy mixing up a tincture while asking me a slew of questions about my lifestyle habits and talking to me about finding balance in my life. I knew I was stressed, but I didn't think that stress would cause me to have night sweats or incontinence or insomnia at the same time. Yes, maybe separately, but *all at the same time*? That didn't seem as possible as the idea that my body was going through some sort of physiological change.

Several different Chinese herbs comprised the tincture he mixed. Dong Qui stuck out to me the most. Dong Qui has been used for centuries to help women with menstrual pain, bloating, and heavy periods. It's also used to help ease menopausal symptoms. Imagine my surprise when, after the first week, I stopped having any hot flashes, slept through the night, and didn't have to race to the bathroom.

Now, I'm not saying that everyone needs to rush out and get some Dong Qui, but I am saying that being dismissed by your physician when you clearly have symptoms of menopause is something to be addressed.

So, how can we, midlife Gen-X women, help ourselves in navigating this menopausal madness?

Step 1: Choose Your Physician Partner

The first thing to do is to make sure your physician is your partner in your health care. Of course, you have to come in ready to do your part in sharing all of your concerns, being open with your physician, and being clear about what you're hoping to achieve. I mean, do you want to kick menopause's ass or what? Even more than that, you have to be willing to change a few bad habits. After all, you can move more, eat foods that are good for your body, lower your stress, and get better sleep to care for yourself and be the healthiest person you can be, which is less about pills and medical treatments and more about how you eat, move, and live.

This partnership is invaluable when it comes to navigating menopause, so if you do not have the right physician partner, now's the time to remedy that. You want a physician who's going to help you find the root cause of what's going on, so you can work on a solution that fits your body and your lifestyle. Unfortunately, there are physicians who practice traditional "here's a pill" medicine. You know the ones—those standard insurance drone physicians who don't take the time to listen to you because they have a daily quota to meet. Even worse are the physicians talking a good game, who say they're interested in going deeper to find out the root cause, but only if you buy their products, plans, and strategies. I don't know about you, but this doesn't align with my approach to healthcare.

There are physicians who are ready to work with you as a partner in a more preventative approach to medical care. These doctors actually sit down with you for more than five minutes so they can dive into all areas of your life with an aim toward uncovering the root of your medical symptoms. It's quite refreshing. These physicians are often called Lifestyle Medical Practitioners, Functional Medicine Physicians, or Integrative Medical Doctors. In fact, there is an entire movement in the medical community to get back to practicing a care model where the goal is to prevent, reverse, and repair. I know, shocker! You need to remember that your physician works for you. They're there to help you get better when you're sick, help you prevent chronic illness, and yes, even navigate all of the symptoms and ups and downs that come with menopause transition. So having a good partner in this health journey is key to how you experience it. Choose wisely.

Step 2: Talk About Menopause Out Loud

The second most important thing when it comes to navigating menopause is to talk about menopause. This isn't Fight Club. We need to talk about menopause out loud. We've spent our lives as women not sharing nearly enough about what we're going through. In fact, I would venture to say you probably have no idea what your mother experienced when she went through menopause.

Am I wrong?

Without other women teaching and guiding us along the way, we come to midlife without much knowledge of what's actually going on with our bodies. It wasn't until recently that I actually sat down with my mom and asked her to talk with me about her menopause transition. She didn't even know the term perimenopause existed. She had a really hard time remembering her own experience, but she did recall finding out about ways of treating symptoms via conversations with her friends. She said that it wasn't easy to get her girlfriends talking until she began sharing her own challenges. Then, and only then, did everyone jump in and share their experiences, too. Together, they learned more and found solutions that none of their doctors knew existed. This is unsurprising, given that menopause education is an incredibly small portion of the educational curriculum of general practitioners. For some, there is literally no menopause education in the course of their training.

There is a serious need for us to talk about our experiences both with each other, and with our medical professionals. This helps us accumulate more data on menopause, the differences between women's experiences, and how the process affects our health. A bonus to sharing more about our experience is that we're able to break the stigma of menopause being a taboo topic and normalize the conversation.

I recently did a TED-style talk on menopause in the workplace and shared that more Gen-X women are leaving the workforce every day due to discrimination. Unfortunately, it's hard to find employers who are educated on menopause and its impact on productivity. If you're in the workforce, you may have noticed your pace has slowed, your productivity is down, you're having trouble focusing and concentrating, and maybe you're experiencing mood swings, brain fog, incontinence, and hot flashes that make the workday painful. The stress of dealing with this natural process while working can drive you nuts. Maybe you feel ashamed about having to run to the bathroom during a meeting, or you're shunned by co-workers who have no idea about what your experiencing. Perhaps you're even anxious about retaining your position. And never mind the backlash that may occur if you dare to request to work from home due to your symptoms!

This lack of menopause knowledge and accommodation in the workplace is a big deal because there are no laws protecting women of menopausal age from the discrimination we encounter in midlife.

Because we don't widely talk about the menopausal transition, it is misunderstand. What we are going through is a natural transformation; but our experience makes others uncomfortable, and therefore has become the butt of jokes. It's happening everywhere we turn—crude jokes at our expense, which have led to increased discrimination. If we don't talk about it and shed a little light on this natural transition in every woman's life, then it remains a mystery to be misunderstood and laughed at generation after generation. There is no better way to take a stand and change this behavior than by talking with each other about what is actually going on and educating out...which is a perfect segue into our next step.

Step 3: Educate and Activate

You can't educate others without first gaining the knowledge yourself, right? So, let's go over some facts.

Perimenopause is brought on by fluctuations in our hormone levels. Our estrogen, testosterone and progesterone levels all dramatically change, which causes havoc with our internal systems. These internal changes can manifest externally in ways that have us all completely freaked.

Let's just start with belly fat. Weight gain and belly fat are the hottest topics when it comes to the menopausal transition women experience in midlife. Although we've been led to believe the pooch is a natural occurrence and is out of our control, there is more to the story. During perimenopause, we'll experience fluctuations in estrogen. As the estrogen drops, we lose muscle mass. Muscle mass is what fuels our metabolism. A reduction in muscle mass causes our metabolism to slow, opening the door for additional weight gain. The average woman can (but doesn't have to) add up to a pound or more each year, and that extra weight can add up quickly. However, weight gain from an estrogen drop isn't inevitable. You can keep your metabolism steady by incorporating or increasing strength training exercise. Strength training builds muscle, regulates your metabolism, and keeps you from gaining excess weight.

Another piece of the menopausal puzzle is where your fat moves or is deposited.

The bummer is that it all goes to your belly.

As our hormones change and we go through the different transitions in perimenopause, all of our excess fat starts to redistribute throughout our bodies. Because estrogen is being depleted, our bodies naturally draw the excess fat to the abdominal region. This is because the body uses excess belly fat to produce more estrogen to make up for the depletion. The production of estrogen happens in the ovaries and adrenals with the help of adipose tissue (fat). The newly deposited fat supports the continued production of estrogen. This is where the menopausal pooch comes into play. The belly buildup triggers us to think we're getting fatter, but we already had this fat on our body. It's all part of the process of getting the body ready to solely rely on fat to produce most of our estrogen after menopause. There's a whole lot of science behind estrogen depletion and changes in belly fat. Mayo Clinic does a great job in explaining the process in their online article, "The Reality of Menopause Weight Gain." [4]

I find it crazy that nobody ever explains it this way. We all laugh and joke about the pooch, but when you understand why it's happening, then you have a better understanding of how to deal with it. Although you can get rid of some of that excess fat, your body needs some fat to keep your estrogen balanced and the body regulated. You can expect that you won't technically lose all of that fat, and that's okay because if we all know this is going to happen naturally to all women, maybe we can stop shaming ourselves and judging others for the little extra belly fat we carry around. Maybe we can even actually learn to love it. Imagine.

The pooch isn't the only external manifestation of internal changes, though. Adult acne is a direct result of the blast of hormonal changes that occur during the phases of menopause. This little skin demon is the worst, because it's been years since we've had to reach for the Seabreeze. The day I got my first midlife pimple at 45, I about died. I had no idea what to do with this lovely gift. I panicked, and it sent me right back to sixth grade. It was funny how quickly I forgot my basic skin care routine and started looking for a quick fix. I was really shook. As soon as I calmed down, I began to research hormonal changes like it was my job (and yes, it is my job).

Menopause brings on other midlife favorites like hair loss, sleep disturbances, incontinence, and something as simple as chin hair (my personal favorite). All of these–like the pooch and acne—are triggered by hormonal imbalance. One thing is consistent in all of my research: correcting the hormonal imbalance affects the body's manifestation of those imbalances. There are lifestyle edits we can make to help balance our hormones naturally or you can seek realignment with a medical intervention like Hormone Replacement Therapy (HRT).

Just remember: it is your job to be a partner in your medical care, so educate and advocate for yourself.

I've presented this information about internal changes causing the external changes to a few groups of women in my community. Surprisingly, it's often met with disbelief, even though I (and millions of other women) am proof that it is true and real.

Here are seven things you can do to help keep your hormones balanced and your transition tolerable:

1. Ditch the Bad Habits

You know the habits helping you dull the pain of midlife? Yep, you do. Drinking in excess, smoking, overeating crap foods, and engaging in excessive drug use are all so damaging to your body and completely throw your hormones off balance even without the help of menopause. I know they are fun habits (until they aren't) that are tough to break, but if you can manage to stop them, you will literally change your life and help your body balance those tricky hormones.

2. Hydrate

I got the hard one out of the way first, so I could make way for the easiest: Keep your body hydrated. About 75% of Americans are chronically dehydrated. You're probably one of them! In fact, take a drink right now!

Good, now we can get down to business.

The average American drinks about 2½ cups of water a day. If that doesn't sound like much, then you're right; it's not nearly enough to keep functioning, let alone help our hormones remain balanced. The human female body is made up of approximately 55% water, depending upon factors like muscle mass and fat. Throughout the day, we deplete our bodies of water with activities like breathing, sweating, waste elimination, and movement. We need to replenish the water we lose to remain in homeostasis (proper function). We are all different in shape, size, activity level, and more, so we should each hydrate based on our own body and its needs. An easy and personalized approach is to drink half your body weight in ounces of water each day. Not coffee, not tea, not energy drinks, not soda, just plain old water. It may seem like a lot at first because you're not used to it, but trust me when I say you'll get used to it. You'll begin to see a difference in your digestion, your skin health, your joints, even your mood. This weight-based approach will help you stay hydrated throughout an average day. However, you'll need to increase your water intake when you lose more fluids than normal, like when exercising or sick. Water is the one thing you cannot live without, and yet it is the one thing people can't remember to do. It is what helps your body function at its optimal level, and that includes helping your hormones stay balanced.

3. Eat Your Nutrients

This brings me to the next thing we can do to balance hormones: Eat nutrient-rich food. That means real food. Food grown in the ground. Fruits. Veggies. Nuts. Seeds. Beans. Whole grains. You also can benefit from lean meats as a good source of protein with less fat. Fatty cold-water fish like salmon provide you with lean protein and the extra added bonus of having omega-3 fatty acids. Omega-3s are necessary to properly nourish the body and to aid in cell function, which protects the heart, eyes, and brain. When it comes to hormones, this healthy little fat balances your blood sugar, which directly increases the production of hormones.

You need plant proteins like tofu, cashew milk, or coconut milk and whole foods full of rich vitamins, minerals, antioxidants, and free radicals.

The current American diet is filled with lab-made, manufactured, formulated, processed foods. Those offerings lack the nutrients your body needs to function well. To make it worse, because the processing of food often removes nutrients, manufacturers must inject it with lab-made vitamins and minerals (basically Frankenstein-ing them back together) to even get approval to sell this as "food." In reality, those offerings are junk and the primary cause of inflammation and chronic illness—not to mention they are hormone disruptors. I won't harp on it too much here, because we'll talk more about this in later chapters, but shifting from processed foods to real food helps to keep your hormones balanced.

4. Move

Exercise goes hand-in-hand with eating nutrient-rich foods. When we move our bodies, nitric oxide is released from the endothelium, the thin layer of cells lining our blood vessels. The role of nitric oxide is to signal the blood vessels to open up the cells in the endothelial walls and release health promoting substances. These substances fight inflammation, lower blood pressure, promote cell growth, regulate hormonal release, and enrich vital organs and systems in the body. With regular exercise you can balance hormones and improve the symptoms felt throughout the menopause transition. The more you move the body, it will take care of itself. Keep the nitric oxide flowing and hormones balanced and you're likely to see your body take better shape.

5. Stay Lean

This leads right into the next thing that we can do to balance hormones, which is to stay lean. Calm down. I did not say or mean "skinny." What I'm talking about is being the right size for your shape. Every body is different.

Different shape.

Different size.

Different muscle mass.

So why do we feel the need to all be within the same weight class or use a BMI as a marker for health? The best thing I've learned throughout my years of study is that your waist size is the best marker for health.

Now I know you just cringed reading that but don't get all crazy and upset. Waist size is something to be mindful of and can help you to be accountable to yourself, instead of the number on the universal scale or in competition with your friend. It's less of a contest between you and others than it is a marker to strive toward as you live a healthier life. A waist measurement of more than 35 inches for women has been linked to poor health and several chronic illnesses. You'll also need to take in consideration your hip-to-waist ratio. This is a good indicator for possible cardiovascular issues and mortality. Ideally, your waist measurement should be equal to or less than your hip measurement.

So how does being lean actually help you balance your hormones? An imbalance (excess or lack) of body fat can throw your hormones off balance all on its own, no matter your age. This, in turn, can cause chronic illnesses or increase your risk for diseases like breast cancer and heart disease. Excess fat can also lead to low libido, insomnia, lack of muscle mass, and memory problems (brain fog!).

6. Sleep Well

If you do all of these things, then this next step is going to be a breeze: Get quality sleep. This is a hot topic especially during menopause because the night sweats and incontinence lead to insomnia. It's a vicious circle. But if you're ditching the bad habits, eating nutrient-rich foods, abstaining from processed foods, moving more, and knocking off a few extra pounds as you lean up, your body will be able to rest easily.

A good night's sleep entails moving consistently through each sleep cycle over a seven-to-nine-hour period. This helps your body replenish, repair, and refresh for each new day. You may not know this, but each night when you sleep, your body completely repairs itself, regenerating cells, processing memories, regulating, downshifting, and completely reviving itself. You're like an electric car being plugged in and recharged while you sleep! This is a required part of being healthy and balancing hormones. Trust me, your body needs all the help it can get to balance these hormones when you're going through the menopausal transition.

7. Manage Stress

There is one more thing within your power that is an integral part of balancing hormones during menopause: Stress management. There is so much to explore and talk about with regards to stress management, so let's give this gem a whole chapter of its own.

Before you go, here are a couple prompts for things you can do to make your midlife and menopause not so manic:

• Write down all of the menopausal symptoms you are currently experiencing.
• Make a list of your medical team with contact information, so you can discuss your experience.
• Ask yourself, what you could be doing to help your body balance its hormones? Make a list.
• Try something new. I'm sure one of those things stands out as something you're willing to try right now.

Chill Out

/'CHil,out/
adjective

1. intended to induce or enhance a relaxed mood.
Ex. *"Why don't you just chill out?"*

2. a period of relaxation.
Ex. *"I'm going to sit here and chill a bit."*

(smoothly managing stress)

Chill out, chillax, take a chill pill, "Relax, Francis"[5]—or better yet, calm the fuck down. Let's address the elephant in the room, the thing we're all dealing with and won't really talk about: stress. If you're finding it hard to take it easy in midlife, well, you are not alone. These days couldn't be more UN-chill.

Take a break from your own stress for a second, sit right back, and allow me to tell you my stressed-out story. It was on a Friday after working an over 60-hour week. I was walking to the parking garage to get in my car and head home to a couple drinks and ease into a relaxing weekend away from work. Right as I opened the door to the garage entrance, I felt a slight twinge in my neck. I grabbed my neck and began to rub it as I said bye to my coworkers and bounced off to the car and drove home. When I arrived at home, I downed the drinks that my husband lovingly had waiting for me. We sat down for a delicious works pizza dinner with extra breadsticks and more drinks; then we watched a movie, and went to bed.

The next morning when I woke, I couldn't even sit up in bed.

Excruciating pain radiated through my neck. The kind of pain that runs down the back, all the way down to the toes. I couldn't sit up straight. I couldn't bend. I couldn't move my head. It was painful just to reach out and grab for my phone. Once I finally managed to sit up, phone in hand, I called my husband, crying. I couldn't move. I wasn't even able to move to go to the bathroom, let alone make breakfast for our son. My husband came home to help, but I had already fought the pain to get through breakfast, throw on some clothes, and get myself on the couch. For the rest of the weekend, I didn't leave my couch. I spent most of my time bouncing between cold packs and hot pads, while liberally applying Arnica and icy hot on my neck until I got the slightest relief and passed out.

On Monday morning, I called my chiropractor first thing for an emergency visit. My husband had to drive me there and help me walk up a flight of stairs. When I tell you it was painful, I actually cried the entire way from my couch to the chiropractic table. After what felt like a lifetime, the doctor asked me two things: How stressed are you, and do you ever drink water?

I stopped to actually think about those questions. I was stressed to the gills. I mean I couldn't imagine being more stressed out. Come to think of it, I don't think I'd ever been that stressed in my life. And as far as drinking water, I couldn't even tell him the last time I'd actually had water. I mean, I took a glass of water to bed every day, but I never actually drank it. If I was being completely honest, I rarely (read: never) stopped to drink water at work, either. Who has the time?

He shook his head, let out a sigh as he sat me down, put a bottle of water in my hand, and shared his assessment. He told me I was suffering from stress-related illness that had locked up my entire body. At some point in time, I had bruised the arch of my foot, which had thrown my ankle and entire body out of alignment. It wasn't a surprise that I felt nothing because my body was completely dehydrated and in a state of shock. It was too busy trying to keep me operable that it had no time for other pain. The pain in my neck was a physical alarm going off.

My body was shutting down due to stress and dehydration.

He asked me if I could take some time off work. I literally laughed out loud. I mean, who was going to do the work? I obliged and compromised internally. After all, I had a team of six who needed my guidance, and I was overseeing eleven multi-million-dollar new build projects, as well as numerous others. So, I planned to take a day to rest, then work from home for the rest of the week.

Or at least that is what I told myself.

I did manage to rest for a good 24 hours. And I got the biggest mug I could find, had one of the graphic design team make me a button to wear around the office prompting co-workers to ask me if I had water lately, and considered the matter addressed.

It took me another year and multiple stress-related incidents before I got shingles and a clue as to what "stress management" actually meant.

I tell you my tale of stress not to get an Oscar, but to let you know that I've been on the other side of stress management and it took me time to realize I had a situation brewing before I actually did something about it. If you're like me, you've spent more of your life stressed out than chilled out. Career, children, husband, being a woman in today's world, and just life—managing all the things is exhausting and nobody taught us how to juggle it all without drinking ourselves to death. We were taught to take it, look like we have it all together, never let them see you sweat, never complain, smile, and be the vision of perfection. Nobody warned us that we'd be dying a slow death inside, while making everything look effortless. It's no wonder we're falling victim to the stress of it all. They stopped handing out Valium like candy, and drinking at lunch is no longer *en vogue*.

So here we are. The Stepford Wife existence is unraveling, and we're finally being honest about how stressed we are. It's time we understand stress, the emotions we feel, the unrealistic expectations, and the effects stress has on us so that we can break this cycle and have it different for our second act.

Nothing describes the sheer panic and anxiety of my stress experience like the movie *Clerks*. Even though watching Dante's day go tits-up sparks a flood of anxiety within me, it's rewarding to see him finally get through the day. Over and over he cries out for relief, "I'm not even supposed to be here today!"[6] but nobody listens. Makes my stomach rise to my throat just thinking about it. This might just be the best representation of what my stressed-out existence felt like. I couldn't catch a break. Funny thing was, I *allowed* it all to happen to me.

Let's get real for a second. Life is filled with stressors. Even something as simple as trying to figure out what you're going to eat tonight for dinner can stress you out if you let it. Stressors can be external (i.e., traffic jam or mean girls), but they can also be internal (i.e., unrealistic expectations or fear). Both can trigger your body's fight-or-flight mechanism. This system works in your favor when you encounter a lion. Your body naturally cycles from alerting you that there is a lion to helping you decide to fight or run, then to you getting away, then to your body relaxing from its excited state to calm because the lion is no longer a threat (or you're dead, in which case you're forever relaxed).

The opposite is true when stressors continue to trigger your system time and time again without any relief. The stress response is triggered and never turns off, causing the cortisol hormone level to elevate and never drop, which in turn creates a chronic stress condition that leads to illness. The research is aligned in how chronic stress is causing chronic illness such as heart disease, obesity, diabetes, anxiety, gut health issues, and fatigue, just to name a few. I tell you all of this not to freak you out but to inform you as to the process and the pain that is stress.

Stress is stress, but just like with all things in life, it doesn't become a thing until we react to it, place meaning on it, and tie an emotion to it. All this is to say that we decide how and if that stress is going to affect us or not.

Say you want to have a more chill experience with less stressors. What would you need to do?

The first thing I recommend is to gain some awareness. Put more simply, get clarity. You have to know what is causing the stress, even if all you can think of is what is right on the surface. You must identify it, and then you'll know how to manage it properly. Don't be fooled. Identifying what is causing your stress takes a little work. In fact, you're looking at a four-step process.

Take a moment and step back from all of the energy around you. Listen and ask yourself what is really causing your stress. If you're like most of us, you will find there are multiple layers to your stress. However, when you start to peel back that onion, you will be able to find greater and greater clarity as to the real root of the problem.

Let me give you a quick example of what it looks like to really get to the root issue. You're super stressed out with all the crazy traffic after work. Ask yourself if it's the traffic or that you are running late to pick up the kids from after-school care. Then ask yourself if the stress is that you are running late or could it be the stress of having to attend a late-afternoon meeting called by your boss for no reason. Then ask yourself if all this stress is the result of the meeting or is it that you gave your boss this update via email, but she wanted it told to her instead. If you continue to keep asking yourself the this or that question, you'll eventually end up with a clear root cause.

When looking at the root cause of your stress, it's important to know what is happening in that moment. When you feel the stress start to build, what are the details? This is where self-awareness comes into the equation. You're looking for how the stress is making you feel physically, mentally, and emotionally.

Once you understand your reaction to the stress, you can then start to understand how you may want that reaction to be different. This one is where we dive deep. You know what is causing the stress and the details about how it makes you feel, but now you get to discover how you really want this to be.

You're not trying to find the solution in this step, you're imagining what could be different with the scenario and how differently you'll feel if it changes.

We're now at the fun part for all the Gen-X Type-A planners. This is where we get to try to solve the problem. I'm not asking you to find one thing only. You're going to make a list of all of the possible solutions. Every last thing you can come up with until you fully exhaust all of your possible fixes and this includes the off-the-wall ideas. Yep, you can brainstorm even the most outlandish ideas. The sky's the limit.

Time to evaluate your list. Here's where it becomes all about you. (I know you love this, you attention-starved Gen-X-er!) You're going to look for solutions. Not just any solutions. We want to keep an eye out for those things you would actually be up for trying. Mark them on your list and put them in the order in which you want to try them. This list is optimal for managing stress in the moment.

You're going to spend some major time in this awareness phase, but it is going to pay off some big dividends. Awareness helps us build the strategy to our healing. It is critical to work from a place of understanding ourselves and what we really want before tackling any of the solutions. When we become fully aware, we can start to build and work toward our vision of having this life go differently than what was handed to us.

Let me share my real-life experience of how these steps have worked in my life. As I mentioned before, my stress hit me physically like a Mack truck. It was when I was diagnosed with shingles and ordered to stay home and rest, that I finally took the time to walk through each of these steps. It was easy to see how the stress was treating me physically, but I learned so much more about myself as I moved from step to step. First, I listed out on a piece of paper how my stress was manifesting in me physically. The list went on and on, but as I wrote everything down, I realized I was mad at everyone, anxious, feeling depleted and trapped. I was mentally exhausted and unable to manage or even see all of the opportunities in front of me.

As I took this first step, I remembered being in a meeting about a project that would boost my career, with an executive team member, and actually saying that I didn't know when I was going to have the time, but I'd add it to my list. What the hell is that?

The more I peeled back the onion by asking myself questions, pulling out the emotions and details, the more I learned. I was taking on more projects to make up for my feelings of inadequacy. I was bottling up my ideas, muting my voice, and keeping my head down so I wouldn't be seen. I was killing myself for a job I didn't even like for people who made me feel small, and I'd had enough.

The next step was where I really saw my blood pressure, cortisol, and stress level drop. As I began to write out my best day and what that would look like, I actually had a sensory experience. It was so real. I was able to fully imagine living a life that felt safe, expressive, joyful, and healthy. I imagined a life where I could set my own schedule and be creative, where people respected and asked for my guidance and perspective. My vision included traveling, cooking, painting, and spending quality time with my husband and family. Once I had this clear vision, it was easy to see what had to change in my life to reach that goal.

When I sat down to brainstorm ideas, the solutions came flying out. Everything from delegating projects to standing at the door to the office building screaming at the top of my lungs before starting my work day. Remember, I said the ideas could be outlandish. When I exhausted my brain, I began to prioritize my list. I determined that while tiny steps could help me make my situation at work more pleasant, what I really needed was to find my purpose in a new direction. I took a little more time to explore my thoughts on pivoting careers, got clear on my life goals, took a few classes to learn new skills, and left my career and old life behind. Now, I'm not saying that everyone needs to quit their job, but that was what I eventually did. These steps resulted in me rising up, removing all of my stressors, completely changing my life, and catapulting me into a beautiful new existence.

Awareness is the big heavy and probably the most important tool to managing stress, but I have others in my toolbox worth sharing.

Creating a routine sets up your day for greatness, lowers the stress, and sets your wellness in motion. Why? Well, routines are consistent, habitual, and not having to spend time thinking what you're going to do next is calming. When you're in the rhythm or the flow of your day, you tend to feel less anxious, more grounded, in control. You're living with intention and leaving space for *time*. Time is the little morsel that we all want more of and stress out when we don't have enough. What does more time give us? A chance to rest, take care of ourselves, make healthy choices, and choose how we spend those extra stress-free moments.

Sit back for a moment and imagine if the important things in your life were on autopilot. Imagine living in the flow, where your life just *is*.

Calms you to your core doesn't it? This is what a life of little to no stress feels like.

It's not about having an impenetrable schedule. Even typing that makes the hair stand up on the back of my neck. It's about having a lifeline to hang onto when things start to get crazy or stressful.

You know you can just go back to your routine and ground yourself. This sense of control that living with a good routine gives you has its benefits. The biggest one is that it forces you to make yourself a priority. Sticking to your routine enables you to avoid those stressful distractions that may present themselves and gives you the ability to set boundaries.

"Boundaries" has been a big buzzword over the past few years and, ladies, let me tell you, they are necessary if we are getting out of here alive. They've been talked about to death, so I'll spare you most of my thoughts. The one thing you need to remember is that boundaries can actually set you free. Having defined limits will keep you from being overwhelmed, stressed, or even upset. Being clear about what you are and are not okay with will allow people to understand your limits. When you protect what's important to you, it will remain the priority. Having boundaries allows you to find the strength to use your voice and say, "Not at this time, but ask me again." Not only do boundaries help you protect yourself, your sanity, and your time, they also help you clearly communicate to others what you are good with and where your limit is. When you have clear boundaries, people will naturally adjust themselves and their behavior to fit you. And your stress levels will automatically lower.

How do I use boundaries? I put on a do-not-disturb on my phone and computer from 10 until 6 each day. No joke. This is what helps me stay on track and get shit done. Those people and their wants and needs of me will be there when I'm done doing what's important to me and my time. Life doesn't have to be met with instant gratification if it is at the expense of your mental health. I view boundaries as self-care, and they help me set realistic expectations in my life.

Another key tool in managing stress is building a good stress-busting squad. Whether you use the term squad, crew, posse, gang, herd, or hookers, it's all the same—a group of women who will support you from friends to family, teammates to co-workers, and beyond. Who can you laugh with, cry with, count on, go deep with, just be with? Who are the ones who really get you and support you anyway? These are the people who should make up your squad.

There is a bigger bonus for all you social butterflies out there. Research shows that being social helps you live longer and reduces stress-induced cortisol release. As a reminder, cortisol is the hormone that does the deep damage to our mind, body, and our soul. Especially as we reach the chronic stress level, when the floodgates are open, and we're rounding the corner on burnout.

Need help putting your squad together? Here's an easy exercise I learned in school to help you narrow down the list. Think about your people and ask yourself:

• Whom do you admire or who is that one person you want to be when you grow up?
• Who really (I mean really) listens to you when you just need to get it all out?
• Who can come up with all the ideas when you need help figuring it out?
• Who has the balls to tell you when you're batshit crazy with love in her heart?
• Who would drop everything and cut a bitch or ride shotgun when you need to make sure you're not crazy?
• Who pumps you up, cheers you on, and adds the spirit fingers with sparkle?

Once you have this list, you have a magical squad of sisters to help you get through anything. If you don't have these people, find them!

Now for the final and difficult task which is to have a little self-compassion. I'm going to say something to you and I want you to write down how you react physically, mentally, and emotionally to it.

Ready?

It is okay if you DO NOT have it all together.

How did that feel? Did it hit to the core, was it a relief, or did you reject it?

Now, we're gonna try something else.

Repeat after me.

Say it out loud.

It is okay if I DO NOT have it together.

Get a little throw-up in your mouth? Feel strange or feel good? There is no right or wrong reaction, so just notice what is happening and how you're reacting. You're probably thinking to yourself, "What does this have to do with managing stress?" It's a valid question.

I refer to self-compassion as showing yourself a little grace, a little kindness. Relieving stress comes naturally when you are kind. A certain calm comes over you and you're able to shift your perspective and see yourself and your stressful situations differently. You'll be less judgmental, harsh, and nit-picky (otherwise known as over-analyzing). You'll focus more on the positive and let the stressful people and situations just disappear. You'll be more in the moment, which will allow you to work through and let go of past stress, as well as stop obsessing on the future that hasn't been written yet. You'll be more focused on and grateful for what you have. Better than all of this is the fact that you'll be able to experience your authentic self, while becoming and loving yourself even more.

With self-compassion, you can start liking and, even better, *loving* yourself. You'll become really present, learn to understand your emotions, gain the ability to calm the flare-ups, learn to be caring and kind to yourself, and ultimately allow yourself how to heal and diminish all those unnecessary stressors.

Focusing on building and practicing self-compassion will also ripple out and affect the way you act towards others. You may even begin to notice your calm being the calm in the storm for them.

I want to wrap up with a summation of what it looks like to live a stress-free life. I saw this one time, I think it was from the American Institute of Stress. It sums up living stress-free so magically that it's become one of those poems I refer to when I start to feel life getting in my way again. It is what motivates me to continue to build a life that is as stress-free as possible.

Your life literally slows down.
You stop wishing for the weekend.
You stop merely looking forward to special events.
You begin to live in each moment and
you start feeling like a human being.

You just ride the wave that is life,
with this feeling of contentment and joy.

You move fluidly,
steadily,
calm,
and grateful.
A veil is lifted,
and a whole new perspective is born.
And this is how you live a stress-free life.

Before you go, here are a couple prompts for things you can do to make your stress more manageable:

• Write down what your typical day would look like without any stress.
• Try a new solution to handling your stress or stressor.
• Update each contact in your phone for every person on your squad list with a magical name and unique ring that corresponds to their magic power.
  • Do one nice thing for yourself today.

Bogus

/'bōgəs/
adjective

1. not genuine or true; fake.
Ex. "The idea of the perfect woman is bogus."

(busting the myth of perfection)

Truth Bomb: I was raised to be perfect. My picture of perfection was painted on using books on charm, poise, posture, and etiquette—learning subtle responses to polite conversation, how to sit properly, not chew with my mouth open, to be seen and not heard. I was highly educated, along with constant reminders to be subservient, penitent, and pretty. Somewhere between June Cleaver and Joan of Arc, but I ended up more like a mashup of *The Breakfast Club*'s Claire (the princess) and Allison (the weirdo).

Anybody else grow up with some sort of bogus idea of what it means to be a woman?

I'm not trashing my upbringing. I mean, I do have great posture and know which fork to use, but because I thought I had to be perfect, I filled up my soul with unrealistic expectations—all of them. The result? A good, long time in working out my worthiness issues, resetting my confidence, and learning to love my authentic self in my fifties. I won't go into all the gory details of my ordeal with perfection, but I think it's good for me to mention that I, too, struggled with this demon and it caused both devastation and massive growth.

Why don't we think we're good enough?

I know some very extraordinary women who can't say a good thing about themselves. For some reason, they don't seem to believe they're good enough. We women have been conditioned to be a walking contradiction—not a harmonious yin-and-yang existence, but a juxtaposition. Living in complete contrast with ourselves in every moment, about everything, and with every action. Our "perfect" is a Frankenstein monster. And the funny thing is that we beat ourselves up over and over because we think we're doing it wrong.

Recently, we've had the rare experience of having the myth of perfection exposed publicly within the movie *Barbie* (2023). There are so many beautiful life lessons to take away from this film, but the one that resonated with most women across the world was the monologue by the character Gloria, played by America Ferrera. When she says, *"You have to be thin, but not too thin. And you can never say you want to be thin. You have to say you want to be healthy, but also you have to be thin."*[7], I actually cried out loud in the theater.

Gloria's words, well Greta's words, provide such intricate insight into the struggle all women go through to be perfect. It aligns us in the fact that we're all exhausted by trying to make a perfect reality and provides us with greater understanding of what happens when you hold a generation of women to this standard of perfection. I don't know about you, but it hit me so hard in the Gen-X lady balls that it needs to be where we begin our conversation.

I've listened to her monologue over and over, even talking about it with my mother on our podcast, in order to force a Boomer-to-Gen-X discussion. We came to the collective conclusion that our perfect generational conditioning has become a subconscious truth. Somewhere in our ancient brains (the part of the brain that encompasses the brain stem and limbic system), passed from generation to generation, over centuries, this has become our norm. Perfection at this level is giving women such mental and emotional whiplash, we don't know... I'll stop there. We don't know. At this point, if you haven't seen the movie or the monologue, put down this book, find it, and watch or listen.

Her last statement is the perfect power punch to the gut. *"I'm just so tired of watching myself and every single other woman tie herself into knots so that people will like us. And if all of that is also true for a doll just representing women, then I don't even know."*

Take a moment and get a tissue before you move on.

This monologue is incredibly powerful. The bitch of it is, we've all been told to be perfect in all the ways Gloria presents. We've been conditioned to feel like we have to be everybody's everything; and while you're at it, you can't have any flaws, you can't have any defects, and you can't show any fear or any emotion around any of it. Often, not only does society hold us to this unrealistic standard, but we hold ourselves to it because we think we have to be what they say. You think you have to be the perfect mom, the perfect friend. You think you have to be the perfect co-worker. You've got to be the perfect wife. Also, there is no clear definition for "perfect" in those roles, as it's different for different people. One thing is clear: "perfect" means a constant struggle for women.

This is a big, heavy topic, and it's hard for those of us who were raised to always be on, people-pleasing, and anything but ourselves.

Let's start with the dictionary definition of perfection to keep us honest. The Oxford Dictionary definition is very eye-opening. It describes perfection as, "the condition, state, or quality of being free or as free as possible from all flaws or defects." Perfection is, "the action or process of improving something until it is faultless or as faultless as possible."

After reading this definition, I wonder why we're not all just bonkers having to live up to this bogus, unrealistic standard of being.

Is it just me, or do you remember perfection being fed to us in a way that was more about being a perfectionist, striving to be your best? Pardon me, but this is complete horseshit. If you live in this world as a perfectionist, you're actually really damaging yourself in ways that you probably never imagined. Ultimately, you'll burn yourself out as you constantly try to hold yourself to these unrealistic expectations, not to mention the shame you put on yourself when you fall short. This self-shaming then sends you into a spiral of worthiness issues, low self-esteem, depression, anxiety, and so much more. It's such a highly toxic situation for you mentally and emotionally, which catapults you into a head space from which some never return.

A perfect place to start (see what I did there?) is to talk about the fact that we are not perfect. A conversation like this is hard because who wants to admit they're not perfect? But the truth is that each of us is flawed. And it's scary to admit that this is not the life we thought it was going to be. It's uncomfortable to be completely exposed and vulnerable with others. We have an innate need as humans to be accepted; and for this we hide what we feel will not be welcomed, usually at the peril of our authentic self.

One thing I know is true: your *authentic* self is already perfect. That's right, girl, you're perfect. The flip side of living or striving for perfection is living in authenticity. It's time you stop trying to be what society says you should be or live up to someone else's idea of what you should be and start being you.

This is where the work happens.

It's interesting to think about why we feel the need to live up to someone else's idea of what or who we should be. Your parents play such an interesting role in introducing you to the idea of perfection. How your parents raise you, what you're told to be, expectations that were set, how your thoughts were guided to develop—all of this defines your idea of perfection. From an early age, your parents make a lasting imprint on you based on their generational experience around this idea or myth of perfection.

Perfection and the generational impact of this way of being left a mark on me. I was told from an early age to look my best to impress others, so people would like me. My mom always told me to be sure to "paint the barn" before I left the house, which meant to put on makeup (or at least lipstick). I took this as meaning that I had to look pretty to be seen, which really screwed with my self-esteem. I learned that if I wasn't pretty and if I didn't look good enough, they wouldn't take me seriously, they wouldn't like me, they wouldn't want to be with me, they wouldn't promote me, and I wouldn't be seen.

I can almost guarantee that my mother heard the exact same thing from her mother, although neither one would ever fully admit to the role this played in my life. After all, I'm sure they didn't mean for it to be taken this way, but that definitely was the meaning I placed on those words.

To be fair, we don't just form this view of ourselves solely based on what our parents say or do. There are others who drive home the myth of perfection too—from friends and teachers to coaches and mentors and beyond. Those other people can leave marks just as deep or at least enhance the marks already created. Our societal norms also feed into the myth that we aren't enough. Wrap all three of these bad dads together, and then you have to decide how this is all going to land with you. That's the kicker and where we do ourselves more harm than good.

Beyond how Gen-X girls were raised, others' impact on our lives, societal expectations, and our warped little brains, we're now dealing with the need to constantly compare ourselves to one another. How could we not, with all the perfect lives being shoved in our face by every social media platform and user adding extra flame to the fire? Don't be fooled, because ninety percent of what you see isn't even real.

The truth of the matter is that "perfect" is a made-up construct that has no merit or real place in our world. **It is unattainable and devastating, but what if we adjusted the definition of "perfect" and redefined our pursuit of it?**

Hear me out. What if we all stopped accepting or demanding perfection of each other and instead valued authenticity?

Well, you'd for sure have to stop lying to yourself, shaming each other, and making up these unrealistic expectations of what it means to be a woman. You might shake up the entire world by removing that cracked mask of perfection and exposing yourself for who you really are, flaws and all. If you begin to value authenticity over perfection, then you need to begin to live your truth as your true self. If you can do this, then you will dramatically change your life by being present and grateful for what you have and who you are, loving yourself, and reducing the stress of having to be perfect and juggle it all with your mouth shut.

Some of the same steps you used to manage your stress actually apply here, too. Awareness of why and how you hold yourself to those perfect but unrealistic expectations is a start. Developing boundaries that allow you to remain authentic and in line with your core values and beliefs is imperative. Surrounding yourself with a squad of positive women who love you for you will keep you grounded. Showing yourself love and kindness can go a long way when you're being vulnerable and authentically you.

It's also helpful to know what feeds this perfectionist mindset, so you can avoid it at all costs. Don't worry, I have a short list.

The lack of honest conversations between women tops my list. Who are we kidding? We're all scared, damaged, making mistakes, failing, and hustling, so why can't we just admit it to each other? If we did, then we could relax, commiserate together, and support one another, knowing that we're all not perfect.

Also, why are we hanging on the Gen-X multitasking trait like it's gold? It's not, and while you may be able to juggle and do all the things, you aren't doing them all well or even getting them all done. Plus, you're burning yourself out and sending yourself down a rabbit hole of failure and shame. Truth is that you can't do it all, nor should you. Stop it!

Last but certainly not least, quick question: Do you spend hours scrolling through social media looking at how great other people seem to have it?

Yeah, same here. Everyone always looks like they're having so much fun "doing life," finding success, on the cutting edge, and they're so beautiful. Let's be honest. Constantly comparing yourself to others is a stress-inducing, anxiety-ridden, demoralizing hot mess— and a total waste of time. While comparison is an innate human trait, it has two sides. On the bright side, comparison can inspire us to grow and learn. However, when we lose ourselves in it and the negativity comes creeping in, it becomes a total drag.

One of the first things I did when I made a choice to live as my authentic self was to un-follow or hide those people to whom I constantly compared myself on my social media. It was a breath of fresh air, and I will never stop recommending it to everyone I meet. It completely took my stress away.

If you're really strong, spend less time scrolling on social media altogether. You'll soon see real change happening in your mental and emotional health. It's incredible how we can make a simple change like this and have a major impact on our lives.

Do me a favor and remind yourself of your unique strengths,

accomplishments, and blessings because, let's face it, you're pretty great. Start small by asking yourself what you can do to feel more like you.

We're all different, but collectively we can all recognize that the pursuit of perfection is a dangerous place to live. Let's spend our time as women building each other up instead of tearing each other down and stop holding each other to these unrealistic expectations of what it means to be a woman. Most important and my final word: In order to be a healthier and happier you (no matter who you are), you must nestle into your own uniqueness.

You can begin by reviewing and completing the following prompts to help you shift your perfect perspective:

• Grab a pen and paper, channel your inner Bridget Jones, and write this line 50 times: I love me, just the way I am!
• Un-follow or un-like social media profiles that cause you to negatively compare yourself.
• Follow or like social media profiles of those who inspire you in a positive way.
• Forgive your past imperfect you and start fresh by doing one thing today that will make you feel more like your authentic self.

Go Postal

/gō/ /ˈpōst(ə)l/
adjective

1. become crazed and violent, especially as the result of
stress.
Ex. *"It's been a day and I'm about to go postal."*

(how to manage your mood)

Shit, life is hard, and it's even harder to contain the sheer anger and
madness that ensues when people aren't doing things our way or the
way we were taught—I'm talking to you, Boomers and Millennials. It's
enough to make you go completely postal.

It could be my midlife hormonal imbalance talking, or it could be
that everyone is stupid. Either way, how do we deal with all of these
free-flowing emotions? Do we stay in the box or lane we were told to
be in until we explode, or do we explore letting go a tad more?

First thing's first, my menopausal midlife maiden, let's talk
irritability and discontent. While there are several side effects to our
hormones being out of balance, we're going to touch on mood swings
and menopausal rage in particular here. Mood swings are the little
menopausal gifts that keep on giving, Clark. They can be a ball of fun
to deal with, especially at the time of life when the "o Fucks Meter"
turns on. Menopausal rage is a thing; and I assure you, you are not

losing your mind. There is a natural explanation for this disruption.

Our hormones are sensitive little ladies. One move up or down from their original resting level can throw your entire system off. Perimenopause causes our estrogen, progesterone, and testosterone levels to change. This hormonal imbalance can also trigger other hormones like serotonin and norepinephrine to be thrown off balance, as well. Because of this change, our happiness meter and how we deal with stress gets off kilter.

I'm not sure anyone really thinks about it, but our hormones go out of wack several times throughout our life cycle and at these different stages in life we deal with physical, mental and emotional side effects as a result. Remember PMS? It begins with puberty and our first period, can happen again with pregnancy, then again when perimenopause hits, and even when we are chronically stressed and burnt out. It's insane to think that you could be compounding the problem by, say, being in perimenopause and being completely stressed out. Like a powder keg, it's an opportunity for a very intense situation and explosion to occur. **So, why doesn't anyone ever talk about what that means, what to expect, or what to do about it?**

My meno-rage has been strong. In fact, I keep imagining I'm trying not to go to the dark side, but the Emperor keeps telling Darth Vader, "the Force (a.k.a. Rage) is strong with this one." For me it happens most often when I'm driving. You haven't seen road rage, until you've seen menopausal road rage. It is no joke. I will get into the car, and I am subconsciously transformed into a road rage manic. I am F-bombing everybody and I'm on full tilt the entire time I'm in the car because nobody is driving right. My poor husband is sitting beside me saying, "It's okay, we'll get there" and I snap back in a low demon voice to say "SHUTTTTTTTT UPPPPPPPPP." Actually, he could say nothing, and I would be like (demon voice again), "Shut your face!" The poor guy is a saint. Unfortunately, I also live in an area of the country with one of the highest concentrations of drivers over the age of 75 who also like to go to happy hour at 3pm each day, so can you say, "Trigger?"

I'll see it coming too, which is the craziest thing of all. I don't want to be this way and yet it's almost like it's happening in slow motion or like I'm having an out-of-body experience. You know the cartoon when Yosemite Sam is boiling over and you can see it coming? His face turns red, sweat starts pouring down the face, and steam starts to rise—just before the whistle sounds and his head blows a complete gasket. Well, that's what I imagine I look like just before I cuss out that little old lady who can't see over the steering wheel. Don't even get me started on when things don't go according to my plan. Whoa!

I'm sure you have some stories too, but you are probably at the point where you want to know what you can do to self-manage your emotional swings.

The thing to look at first is how you want to balance those hormones. There are several options for you to choose from starting with Hormone Replacement Therapy (commonly referred to as HRT) to natural alternatives and healthier lifestyle habits. More and more physicians and specialists alike are recommending eating less processed foods, getting quality sleep, continuing to be active, and finding a way to calm yourself that fits into your lifestyle. They've been doing more and more research on the calming and balancing affects of yoga and meditation for stress relief, but also for balancing hormones throughout the menopausal transition.

Once you decide how you want to balance your hormones, you need to figure out what's triggering your mood swings. This information can be valuable when deciding how to manage everything from a minor flare up to eliminating the trigger entirely. Like I mentioned, one of my triggers ended up being traffic. Once I identified the what, then I identified the how. I realized that I wasn't half as stressed or triggered to rage if I left the house 10 minutes earlier than I normally would. Allowing myself more time, I was able to calm down and enjoy the ride as they say.

Finding something to help you calm yourself in the moment is also a valuable step. A friend of mine taught me a great technique to get myself in check. She said to **HALT**. Check to see if you're **H**ungry, **A**ngry, **L**onely, or **T**ired. Sounds easy enough, you could just need to eat something or lower that caffeine intake (I'm talking to you, you little coffee tweaker); It may be that you're upset and angry at something or someone; Maybe you need a hug or just a good friend or therapist to listen; What about taking a little respite to help you turn that exhausted rage enhancer around. Even taking a moment to slow down and HALT will start the calming process.

My go-to is taking a breath. A simple breathing exercise can go a long way and is one of the top ways to reduce stress quickly. Three deep breaths in through the nose on a count of four, out through the mouth on a count of eight can do wonders for your mood and your hormone levels. When you find the technique that works for you, you'll be empowered to self-manage your way to through midlife and beyond.

I'll leave you with this one last quick pro tip: Dehydration throws off those hormones too, so lift up your glass and hydrate that rage away.

Use this moment and these prompts to begin to manage your menopausal mood swings:

• Make a list of all the moods you're experiencing in midlife, along with each trigger
• Have a conversation with your spouse or close confidant, so they know what to expect when your hormones begin to rage—there is peace and understanding in the knowing
• Brainstorm all the ways you can calm yourself in the moment of emotional distress
• Next time you stop at a red light, take that moment to take a few deep breaths to get you started on a calming practice

Trippin'

/trip-in/
verb

1. acting a fool, thinking crazy thoughts, or are maybe high.
Ex. "You must be trippin' if you think I'm going karaoke by myself."

(resetting expectations)

This may be the hardest chapter I've had to write for this book. I think it's because, if I had to label it, I've been straight trippin' about writing this book. Yep, it's true, I'm in a swirling black hole of doubt. After all, writers are these superhuman intellectuals that hide away somewhere, spending years working on and gathering all of their insightful thoughts only to spend even more time putting them on paper. They live for sharing their life's work.

I hadn't even said yes to writing this book when I had already run through this scenario in my head. I basically set myself up with the unrealistic expectation that this was how a writer was and it was not me. I was sure this experience was supposed to be something completely different from what I was going to be able to have, so there was no way I was a real writer. The worse thing was that I had begun to talk myself out of putting anything on paper, because who was going to want to read anything I had to say? I've been plagued with impostor syndrome ever since.

One afternoon, something changed. I was talking with a friend of mine, who's a therapist and a health coach, explaining my swirling brain and my doubts about authoring a book. I told her how worried I was that I wouldn't have anything to say and no one to listen. We started peeling back the onion on all of my issues with worthiness and doubt. How I had kept myself small for years, not wanting to fail while trying to fit into everyone's idea of who I should be and how I should live. Then it happened. She asked me what it would be like if I did write this book, if I did succeed, if I put it all out there and people read it. I stopped in my tracks and imagined you reading this very chapter and smiling because you recognized something in my story that resonated with your life. And so it began.

I got to work right away and began breaking down those unrealistic expectations I had created about being an author. More important, I began to rewrite and reset expectations that fit me, the life I live, and the vision I had around authoring this very book. I learned a great lesson that I feel every woman should know, or at least think about, as she navigates this midlife transformation.

Let's go back before we go forward. If you stop and think about it, Gen-X women have had some pretty intense and high expectations to live up to. Even more so when you consider the fact that we've grown up in a world where we have no equal rights to help us achieve even the smallest societal expectation.

In case you forgot, we were taught to be perfect (see Chapter 3). Enough said. If we're doing our due diligence, we would have to assess societal expectations placed upon women, which takes us right back to the Barbie monologue from our discussion on perfection. The myth of perfection itself is a bundle of unrealistic expectations for women physically, mentally, and emotionally. From what career path we should choose to how and who to marry, how to raise our kids, what activities are proper, and how to keep house and nurture friendships, we have to elegantly juggle it all. Funny thing about Gen-X, women of our generation have also been told fight the power, fuck the patriarchy, down with the man, and be independent as fuck. After all, as Annie Lennox says, "Sisters are doing it for themselves!"[8]

If you choose to accept it, we've kind of been set up for failure from the get-go. We were told life is hard, then you die[9]; When the going and gets tough, the tough get going[10]; You want it all, but you can't have it, it's in your face, but you can't grab it[11]; Shit happens[12]. All singing the same song, you have to persevere, grind it out, grab for the brass ring, take control, and even fight your right to party[13]. Exhausting at best, trying to live up to all of these expectations and get through what life hands you at the same time.

I don't know about you, but I've been disappointed throughout my life by trying to live up to unrealistic expectations of how a situation, experience, person, place, or thing would play out. I was left frustrated, feeling like a worthless piece of crap, angry, tired, disappointed, and ultimately jaded by life. Unrealistic expectations abound and most are of our own making. The problem is, we aren't setting ourselves up for success, we're straight setting ourselves up. Why? Because we want to belong, we want people to like us, we see others doing it and we think we need to do it all too. We listen to what "they" say, and we jump in full tilt. It wasn't until my late forties and early fifties that I realized I could change my expectations. This shift has helped lower my stress level, improve my mood, and enhance my life as a whole.

For years I just went along with what I thought was expected of me. Believe me, I had thoughts and dreams, but I let myself be guided by people I looked up to, well-meaning as they were, when they advised me about my career choices, my relationships, and even my hairstyle from time to time. I began to put a priority on what I felt other people would be happy with or proud of, instead of living out my dreams and daring to jump. I recently found a poem I feel best describes what I was going through. It's called "Breathe"[14] from *Talking to the Wild* by Becky Hemsley.

> *She sat at the back and they said she was shy,*
> *She led from the front and they hated her pride,*
> *They asked her advice and then questioned her guidance,*
> *They branded her loud, then were shocked by her silence,*
> *When she shared no ambition they said it was sad,*
> *So she told them her dreams and they said she was mad,*
> *They told her they'd listen, then covered their ears,*

And gave her a hug while they laughed at her fears,
And she listened to all of it thinking she should,
Be the girl they told her to be best as she could,
But one day she asked what was best for herself,
Instead of trying to please everyone else,
So she walked to the forest and stood with the trees,
She heard the wind whisper and dance with the leaves,
She spoke to the willow, the elm and the pine,
And she told them what she'd been told time after time,
She told them she felt she was never enough,
She was either too little or far far too much,
Too loud or too quiet, too fierce or too weak,
Too wise or too foolish, too bold or too meek,
Then she found a small clearing surrounded by firs,
And she stopped...and she heard what the trees said to her,
And she sat there for hours not wanting to leave,
For the forest said nothing, it just let her breathe.

This poem hit me deep and really aligned with my own experience. One day everything changed for me. I woke up and finally asked myself what was I doing with my life and who was I doing it for? I had lost my path and my purpose somewhere along the way. If I'm honest, I've had a few moments in my life where I crawled out of my box and shifted my life for the better. However, like the cycle that is life, I ended up trying to fit the mold again in that new spot, and then I'd do it all again. It was always like an energetic force pushing me forward and out of the shackles of the box I'm crawling out of, and it seems to be working in my favor and getting me one step closer to my authentic self, purpose, and path.

Years ago, I was in an intensive leadership training program. It was a weekend immersive experience where we all got very vulnerable in order to get in touch with our authentic selves or at least open the door a little more on who we were. There were several eye-opening moments to that training, but one thing has stuck with me for years. One of the mentors in the training asked me to think about lowering my expectations and approaching everything with a higher commitment. Although I've made some adjustments, I never really understood what that statement truly meant until recently. Lowering expectations doesn't mean you aren't making a goal or setting a standard for yourself. It means you're being realistic, starting small, setting attainable goals, setting yourself up for a win. The higher commitment comes as you reset those expectations.

The whole thing with resetting expectations is that you have to get real. The more realistic the expectation, the more attainable it becomes. You have to be present in an authentic head space, but you also have to understand and know your strengths, skills, and vision for a life well lived. It also helps if you look at the world from the positive perspective.

The worldwide COVID pandemic is the most extreme but easiest way to show you what I mean about resetting expectations. We were all forced to reset our expectation about what it meant to work a full-time job. As Gen-X children, we grew up in an era where you were expected and excited to work a 9-to-5 job (thanks, Dolly Parton). The goal being to find a job, get your ideas seen and heard to impress, move up the ladder after years of service, and retire in style. Maybe you'll even find a super successful and incredibly handsome partner that you met by chance at a bar who turns out to be your co-lead on a big project. Oh, wait! That's *Working Girl.* Anyway, the reality is your workday looks more like 8 to 7 with little to no breaks, you've had to claw your way to the top, repeatedly proving yourself in spite of your success; and most likely you've job-hopped to reach the next level on your executive dream.

This unrealistic expectation eroded, along with the entire system, with one global pandemic. We had to adjust our lives and our expectations to fit the new reality. We were faced with the extreme levels of juggling work and home life to make everything fit into a 24-hour day. Working from home meant no commute time needed, but it also made for more distractions and added daily responsibilities. It was overwhelming for most of us, but the beauty was in the shift in expectations that collectively happened. A 9-to-5 workday ended up looking more like 7 to 8, then 10 to 12 or 3 to 6, rounding out with 8 to 10. We reset expectations and approached work with an "I'll get to it when I can be my most productive and nobody else needs me" perspective. Some of us also had the privilege of working outside in nature more, taking conference call meetings while on a walk, eating healthier home-cooked meals, taking longer lunches, or sitting down to dinner with the family. Whatever your reality was, you had to shift your perspective and reset expectations based on the pandemic reality, thus lowering the bar so you didn't go crazy.

For the first four months of the pandemic, I failed at resetting anything. In fact, my days intensified, and I was drowning in complete and utter burnout. I allowed myself to be guided by the example other burnouts were showing me. I was told I had to always be on, available for anything anyone needed, and my job was my life. I imposed additional unrealistic expectations on myself and taking on the role of doing all the grocery shopping, meal planning, cooking, and entertaining—or at least orchestrating the planning of everyone else's downtime. I mean, what could go wrong with that? It was all magically supposed to be great—even Utopian, right? It felt as if I needed to control everything, in order to feel safe and secure. However, that didn't work out well at all. I ended up with a crazy case of shingles and doctor's orders to stop everything. I honestly didn't know what to do with myself at one point. I had been running at such a high intensity level for so long that, in order to heal, I needed to find a way to disconnect, to get back to me and what I enjoyed out of life. It reminds me of the movie *Office Space*, when Peter Gibbons wakes up and realizes he doesn't give a damn about those freaking TPS reports. Don't even get me started on how therapeutic it would have been to give that fax machine a boot party. I needed to get out of my current reality, but how?

I happened to be doom scrolling on my phone one afternoon while I was recuperating, and I noticed the local art museum was giving an online virtual tour led by the curator of a new exhibit. My body immediately calmed, and I knew this was what I needed. I spent an hour and a half on a Zoom with three strangers, immersed in the moment, talking all things art, and forgetting about the rest of the world. It was glorious.

The next day, I picked up a book and began to read again. It had been a long time since I just read a book for pleasure, and thank god it happened to be *Untamed* by Glennon Doyle. I related so much to her trained cheetah and the wild that lived within. My heart was bursting with a need to be set free. Set free of the need to control everything around me to feel safe, set free of the expectation that I had to turn my life upside down for a paycheck, free of the expectation that I had to be a corporate drone to be successful, free of the expectation that my needs came second to everything and everyone else, free of the expectation that I had to leave myself behind to be what the world wanted or what I thought they wanted of me. I was ready to run wild!

I began to pull apart all of the external pieces of my life that were eroding. I began to emerge out of my little box and regain some of what made me, me. I explored my career, what had led me here, and what went wrong along the way. More importantly, I remembered that happiness and love were what life was all about. I took baby steps into a new reality of living for happiness and love. I went slowly, one day at a time, exploring the real me and the life I longed to be living. I lowered my expectations around work and what I was willing to give each day, shaping new more realistic goals I could actually attain before dinner. I began to move through my day with less stress as my commitment shifted from having to get everything done to achieving happiness. I was reshaping and setting up my life for what I needed, happiness and love. By focusing on these two core values and aligning my day to achieve them, I made it impossible to have a day without being happy and feeling the love. I won't lie, this actually took me out of my corporate existence and transformed my life in all areas, but I made my life worth living again by resetting my own expectations, prioritizing my values, and getting out of the negative nest I had built for myself to start viewing life from a more positive and grateful place.

One thing I know is true, stressing yourself out for someone else's reason, trying to reach an unattainable expectation, and failing over and over again will only end in regret, low self-esteem, physical, mental, and emotional harm. Life may not always turn out as you planned. More than likely, it will turn out totally different than what you expect, so remember, the only thing constant is change and life is always changing around you.

So how do we change and reset expectations?

It helps to know where these expectations are coming from. Are they expectations derived from societal norms or are they personal, of our own making? Expectations usually come from a vision we have of how we want a situation to play out or an outcome we think should happen, but they also come from a need we may have or a way we can benefit from a situation. The negative emotional response that happens when we don't get our expectations met, well, that's where the disappointment, anger, and frustration kick in to stress us out and send us down a negative thought pattern or a full-blown spiral.

Once you know who's responsible for setting the expectations, then you can work on changing them.

Whether an expectation is set by society or a limiting belief you possess, you can reflect and review it through a series of questions. Ask yourself...

- Does holding this expectation as truth serve me or stress me?
- Is this expectation realistic?
- What am I getting out of holding myself to this expectation?
- Is living to this expectation working in a positive way for my life?
- Does this expectation align with my values and beliefs?

When you have the answers to these questions, let those be your guide to changing your current situation to something more grounded and optimistic. We need to base our expectations in reality and within sight of what is good and working in our lives.

The real first step then becomes creating an alternate expectation that is more realistic, aligns with your values and beliefs, and helps you actualize your vision for your ideal life. Think about what is guiding you and driving you to do what you do. When you have a better understanding of your standards, your motivations, and your needs, you will gain clarity on what you hold dear. Therefore, we need three things to move forward in resetting expectations to be more realistic and have a positive impact our lives: a clear vision, an understanding of what we value, and the strength to let go of our own unrealistic expectations we carry with us and grow.

Gaining awareness is the key to most changes we'll make in our lives, but this time you're going to use that awareness to determine a vision of what you want your life to look like. **Time to create a**

vision.

Since the time of the ancient Egyptians, we've been creating vision boards, vision statements, writing motivational checks to ourselves, building dream boards, working on manifesting, and using the law of attraction to reach for the stars. In the mid-80s, we were gifted with the Oprah Winfrey Show, and Oprah loved her some self-help, vision creation, laws of attraction conversations. I think this was the first time I had ever heard of a vision board, but there is one thing I know for sure. Having a vision for what you want your life to be will give you clear direction on how to get there. I've studied vision creation and the importance of this method in gaining clarity and awareness with regards to health and wellness. However, having a vision will also help you in other areas of your life, including ensuring your expectations are realistically aligned with your best life.

Let me give you an example. If you're feeling like your career has become stressful, and you don't feel you are living your best life, think about why you ended up at this job in the first place. Explore the path you took, every twist and turn, that led you here to this very moment. Hopefully this is what you were looking for, but if not, then explore why not. Maybe you'll find you ended up here because of someone else's expectations of you, or maybe you got yourself here; but it isn't living up to your expectations. Keep peeling back the onion, asking yourself *why*. Why is the eternal question that always points to the root cause. This may sound very similar to how we approach dealing with our stress; and you would be right, it is. Getting to the root of the situation helps us understand where we need to go from here. Having a clear vision provides us with the direction for the change, in order to get us there.

You can create a vision for yourself in a variety of different scenarios using several tools and tactics. You can use charts, questionnaires, online programs, a good old paper and pen—but whatever you do, it is helpful to put together a representation of your best life for reference when changing expectations. For me, I wrote a story about my best-case scenario day and then pulled out the important nuggets to create a vision statement that I used as a divining rod for changing my life. Whatever your vision ends up being or looking like, it is important to have a vision—so you don't lose yourself in unrealistic expectations again.

Now, let go of everything you know. Stop defining your life by what you may have done in the past and what others may have told you. An easy way to do this is to know what you value in life and align everything you do with making these values a reality. For example, I valued happiness at my lowest point, so I aligned everything in my life with an end goal of being happy each day, even when taking the smallest steps. I let go of everything else and focused on what led me toward happiness. Every expectation I had became about happiness. **In order to do this, you need to know your values.**

An easy values exercise I've used in the past is to imagine or remember a time when you felt empowered, really seen, fulfilled, in the flow, like everything was working at a high vibration. Get down into the details of what you can see, feel or hear in that moment. Think about why it was so special, what you were doing, and who you were with. Really nestle into that incredible moment, so you can really feel it with all your mind, body, and soul. Pick at least three things out of that moment that were the most important in making you feel so great. There might be more, so not to worry, write them all down.

When you're ready to come out of your head, breathe and smile as you look over the list you've created. If you had to number those important things, which one would be most important to you now? Take a moment and number them in order of importance. If you're working with a train of thought, you'll want to narrow that sentence down to one word. For example, if you said, "One of the most important things in my moment was to be surrounded by people I love and trust," then you would want to narrow that thought down to a word like "Connected" or "Social," depending upon what was truly important about that moment and how those people were supporting you. With your list, you'll want to focus in on the top three to five values you've identified.

Now is the tricky part, where you identify if those values are represented in your life right now. An easy way to look at it would be to determine if you are spending your time, energy, or even money toward making those values a priority in your life. Don't worry of shaming yourself if they are not being actualized, because the next step is actually exploring how you can bring those into your life more.

Like I mentioned before, understanding what's important will allow you to create expectations that will align with your values and help to make a more positive impact on your life. In working these values into your life more, you may see a big change in perspective and increased joy. **You just have to give yourself time to learn and grow—It takes grace.**

This means you must let go of the notion that other people are going to live up to your expectations about how they should act or be. You have to get real. It's a fantasy that someone else will act the way you would act or the way you expect them to act. Bottom line is that they are not you. The same is true for a situation. It's unrealistic to expect that a situation or experience will go the way you thought or want or dream it should. You can't control them, nor can you control other people; it just doesn't work like that here in reality.

One thing is true, when your expectations are bigger than reality, you lose sight of what you actually have in the present and all the great things happening within your life. The more realistic the expectation, the more grounded in the present you can be, allowing yourself to be grateful for what is working. This means you have to change your mindset. Shift yourself and your efforts on creating an alternate expectation that is more realistic, aligns with your values and beliefs, and helps you actualize your vision for your ideal life. You just might begin to discover your natural talents, skills and abilities while building on that strong foundation.

As new situations arise, you should ask yourself what you expect out of them and then check yourself to see if that is a realistic expectation. When something doesn't go your way, no need to stew on the negative. This is a time to look at what was good about it. Then you can use that knowledge to reset for the next time you find yourself in a similar situation. You're learning and adjusting in order to grow and have it better next time. Basically, it comes down to becoming more aware of your expectations and how they change your feelings toward your own reality. This one act will set you free from the disappointment and stress that comes from holding onto unrealistic expectations.

You're here, so why not use these prompts to reset some expectations this week?

• Take a moment and think about what a perfect day would look and feel like. Identify one expectation that is holding you back from having that day, and let it go.
• Write down one negative thing about your current situation; then rewrite that one thing as a positive in your life.
• Ask yourself, what is the one thing you value right now above all else? Write that down and hang it at the office or at home as a constant reminder of the end goal.
• Identify one of your magical talents, something you can do really really really well. Try to use that talent this week to move you closer to your identified end goal.

Word

/wərd/
exclamation

1. used to express agreement.
Ex. "I need to get rid of my stress. Word."

(finding harmony)

Who else is sick and tired of trying to achieve the magic unicorn, work/life balance? Can I get a "Word"?

I remember watching the movie *Baby Boom* (1987) and being in awe of the character J.C. Wiatt as she navigated the work/life balancing act of a "Tiger lady" executive and full-time mom. It was complete chaos, but in the end she got her career on track, made time for new love, and perfectly bringing up her new child. Hollywood delivered a complete fairy tale of a woman who struggles and changes her entire life to "have it all." Entertaining movie (I love it), but a complete bill of goods being sold to all the naïve Gen-X women who watched. Talk about unrealistic expectations.

We've all been conditioned to believe that we have to strive, survive, struggle, claw, conform, and suffer to reach that state of thriving, but that's all a crock. There is no way we can possibly achieve some static ideal of life. Like somehow we'll reach a pinnacle where nothing changes, and we're just required to keep it balanced as we move forward. The Greek philosopher Heraclitus said, "the only thing constant is change," [15] and he's absolutely correct. The beauty of life is in its ups and downs, ebbs and flows, changes, and shifts. There's nothing that is consistent or balanced about life, and that's the beautiful part of living. Because we never know what's happening or where we're going or how it's gonna turn out, when we are always trying to control the outcome or keep it balanced, we're just perpetuating the unbalanced nature of it all. It's so stressful when we try to control or keep change from happening. After all, constant change is a fundamental truth.

It's also true that life is full of unknowns. The future hasn't been written yet, so there's always the chance of it changing based on an idea, new thought, or a shift in perspective that leads to astronomically different pathways. It's not as if you're never going to change your mind or come up with a new idea. We're always iterating, having new experiences, taking on new beliefs, and finding value in new ways of being. It's impossible to control, and no way can you put that genie back in the bottle.

Heraclitus went on to say in his writing, "opposites coincide." Similar to the Yin and Yang principle of Chinese philosophy, this interconnectedness of competing energies is another fundamental that is hard to control or keep consistent. The interplay of these opposites depends on each other. The shifts are part of life. I'm not sure you would even call this balance. I wouldn't even say that work and life are opposites. In fact, work is something you do in life, so they're actually more integrated than opposites on the teeter-totter.

I'm going to get really philosophical here for a moment, but I swear I have a point. Think of light and darkness. The moon rises, just as the sun sets, day after day. One is the opposite of the other, but without the light we wouldn't know the darkness. It's not balance at play as they are working in tandem. What we're seeing is a harmony, an appreciation both light and darkness have for each other as they fluctuate or change naturally.

Why am I going into all of this? The balancing act we're told to achieve. The striving, surviving, struggling, clawing, conforming, and suffering—all in the name of the Thrive (aka Balance)—is so completely stressful and causes us to try to live up to unrealistic expectations and nearly kill ourselves in the process.

Throughout all of my searching, learning, and experiences to find balance, I've actually found something so much less stressful and easier to achieve. I've found that life is all about being harmonious. Finding harmony in this existence sparks all the joy and warmth. Even the sound of this simple word is pleasing and calming to the soul. So, I am here to relieve the stress and unrealistic expectation of ever finding any sort of work/life balance. Listen up... You can stop trying to achieve work/life balance. I know it sounds crazy and counter to everything you've ever been told, but it's true.

This is a shift in perspective, similar to how we just shifted expectations. We're going to look at the world from the positive perspective instead of the negative approach to life. If balancing work and life is not the goal, what is?

Now, this is my own take on life, but I feel it is a much better approach than the stressful balancing act we've all been trying to achieve. It's still aligned with the principles and dimensions of well-being, but it's a way to ground yourself in a place where everything that happens in your life will now be in harmony with your core. Everything that you do in your life, decisions you make, what you take on or let go of, the people you surround yourself with, goals you make, and how you live should be aligned with your values. This is something that people don't often think about, and that's because traditionally you probably haven't been taught to prioritize your values as a rule. However, if you can shift your perspective and begin to root your life in your core values, it will create harmony.

Where do you begin?

I love this part of the journey, because it's always a true lightbulb moment. There are online tests, worksheets, and schools of thought, like Myers&Briggs, VIA, or Preventative Index Behavioral Assessment, that can help you in figuring out what your values and beliefs are. Choose one that resonates with you and how you want to explore your values. Remember everyone is different and has different experiences. Don't compare yourself to your BFF, because you two are different at the core and value different things. What is true for you is probably not going to be true for your friend, your mom, your partner, your coworker. We're all different.

If you choose to take an online test or an assessment for your values or beliefs, great! If you find a practice and a way to do it that works for you, fantastic! In the case that you don't want to spend the time googling your options, I'm going to share the quick and easy way I've been taught to determine values. Take your time and have fun exploring this technique.

Make sure to sit down in a place where there are no distractions and no chance of any interruptions (if that's even possible these days). Take a few good deep breaths to center yourself and become present. Now, imagine if you will a time when you may have felt your best. A time when everything was flowing, going your way, and had you feeling like you were vibrating at a high level of happiness. Begin to focus in on the details of that particular moment. Ask yourself more detailed questions like: What was happening? Where were you? Who was with you? What were you doing? How did you feel? Was there a sound or a smell you can remember? Get real and dive into that beautiful moment.

Once you've made a few mental notes of all the important pieces of that moment, you can sit back and pick out at least three things that resonated or were most important in that moment. I know there was a lot going on, but I'm sure you had at least one feeling that made you smile. Make sure you continue to breathe and smile as you write those things down that really mattered. Take a look at your list and pull out at list three (your top three) and rank them in order of importance. You may have to finesse them a bit but you should have a list of three values you hold dear.

Let me give you an example. If I start to think back to a time in my life where I felt I was living my truth and being my authentic self, it would be one of my first two years of college. I was in art school, working in retail and modeling, surrounded by friends from high school and those who I met in class (a real international crowd). I was drawing or painting most days and sitting outside to get inspiration from nature. I was going to museums and drinking in all the knowledge that I could about art and artistry. I was living at home, so I felt secure and safe and happy and provided for. I just remember it being sunny and me taking a lot of walks outside and really being connected.

Now, if I had to pull out the important pieces of that scenario, the biggest one that resonates would have to be having the ability to be creative. The second one for me would be the abundance that I felt being able to live at home and be surrounded by such positive and beautiful things and people. The third thing would be that I was making my own schedule and spending more time on myself, on my purpose, and I wasn't worried about living up to someone else's idea of what I should be.

After finessing each of these a little bit further, I would break each of those three thoughts down into a one word value. For me, the values I pulled from this deep dive are creativity, abundance, and authenticity. Those three, in this moment of my life as I write, are on my values list. True story! This is pretty powerful stuff, and when I start to look at how I am living my life, I can see clearly how my values are being respected and prioritized. I am completely grateful every day for what I have and who I am. I get to be creative with my design projects and writing this book. Even better, I authentically spend my time doing what I know I need to be doing, rather than doing what someone else thinks I should be doing. Pure bliss.

Ask yourself, how are your values showing up in your life currently? Where are you aligning with your values and what areas of your life are not in alignment?

The important thing to remember is that you need to find a way to bring your values into what you're doing in your day-to-day life. When you align your life and your choices with your values, you won't have to struggle or stress. You'll be in perfect harmony without even trying.

One thing to remember about living in harmony is that life is constantly changing, and that also goes for our values too. So it makes sense that you may need to do this type of exercise or assessments of what you value at each unique stage in your life. Getting clear on your values now will help you get out of your own way and started on the journey to live a healthier and happier life.

One more for the road, use these prompts to get you started toward living a more harmonious life:

• Take a quick inventory and ask yourself, "Am I living the life I want to live?"
• Write down what you wish you could do everyday for the rest of your life.
• Brainstorm two things you can do right now in your life to work each of your identified values into your current lifestyle.
• Think and reflect on what you learned about yourself after doing the values exercise.

Gnarly

/'närlē/
adjective

1. difficult, dangerous, or challenging.
Ex. "What a gnarly week."
2. very good.
Ex. "That was one gnarly jam session."

(embracing positive vibes)

I'll admit it, sometimes it's totally tough to look on the bright side of life. Life can be pretty challenging, but if you spin that perspective around, it's like Spicoli says, "Gnarly, Dude!"[16] That one's for all you *Fast Times at Ridgemont High* fans.

There's been so much research behind the benefits of positive thinking and having a positive outlook on life. People who are optimistic tend to be more satisfied with life, they've been found to live longer, they're happier, and they even have the ability to lower the risk of chronic illness. Not to mention the fact that they can deal with stress on a totally different level. Positive thinking has become a movement of manifestation with the idea that living in abundance and thinking positively can change the course of your life.

What I found interesting is that positive or more optimistic people live differently from people who are more negative or pessimistic. I guess that makes sense because if you're always thinking negatively, then you're more than likely living with a negative mindset, where you internalize words and actions in a negative way, you self-shame, you blow things out of proportion, and more than likely you're intent on being perfect, which has its own drawbacks. However, a person who lives with a positive mindset doesn't dwell on the negative. They automatically shift perspective, they're kind to themselves, and they tend to practice healthier habits as a result of treating themselves better. They surround themselves with positive people and support systems, they give back, they are more confident, and they have a totally different way of living and viewing the world.

When I was going through my training at Mayo Clinic, we did a practice together using a Loving-Kindness Meditation. We happened to be studying an interesting experiment by Stanford University in which college students where asked to do a 10-minute meditation daily for 6 weeks as part of a study. The focus of the meditation was to have you focus on harnessing love for yourself and for others through a visualization of you transmitting that love and kindness out to someone in your immediate atmosphere, out a little further to someone in your circle, then to those in your neighborhood, and finally out to the community at large and the world.

The researchers found that after the set timeframe, the participants tended to be more empathetic and compassionate, but they also found those students to have an increased social connection. In layman's terms, they were doing more volunteer work and helping in the community at large more by working with non-profit organizations. They also noticed participants being less critical of themselves and others, more confident, and more optimistic. Honestly, the more I did this meditation and practiced sending positivity out to the world, the more I was really impacted too.

Because of this experience, I've come to believe that if you shift your thinking and view things more positively, then you really will make a huge impact—on not only your life, but on the lives of those people around you, those you interact with on a daily basis, and those people around you that you haven't even met yet. It's a ripple effect.

So what does it look like to shift your thinking and practice a more positive approach to life?

Well, it's very simple. It's the difference between looking at the world with possibilities and looking at the world at its worst. It's also in alignment with the growth and fixed mindset paradigm, which you may have heard about at the office. It's the new trendy conversation. To recap, if you have a growth mindset you're open to opportunities, you're developing, changing and growing. A person who has a fixed mindset is someone who already feels like they're tapped out, that this is their best, that there is nothing they can or have to learn.

Now, how do we shift our perspective?

When shifting to take a more positive approach to life and outlook, you're opening yourself up to all the possibilities life has to offer. You're open to new opportunities, you're ready to learn and grow. You see something that maybe didn't turn out the way you thought, but instead of going down the spiral of negative thoughts, blame, and internalizing, you look at that moment or experience as an opportunity. In order to do this, you must shift your perspective, reframing the experience. This is a skill that can be learned. You know how you've met those people who are just positive all the time? Kind of on your nerves, right? But the beauty of it is, they live at the different level of this existence of positive mental and emotional experience.

You need to remember that shifting your perspective is not about numbing or avoiding the emotions of an experience when it is negative. You have to feel those feelings and deal with those emotions. Let me give you an example. You are on the executive track at the company, but after a series of pretty great interviews with all the department heads, you get passed over for the promotion and take a moment to grieve that fact that you did not end up getting the job. You have to process the feelings of anger, sadness, envy, the not-enough-ness, but instead of going further down a spiral of negative internal talk, the idea is that you would find an opportunity in it or something to learn from within the situation.

In the case of not getting the promotion, maybe you would learn that there are some other leadership skills you could develop. Maybe you learn that there is a better position opening up or another path you can take, a better path for you. You could internalize it as "What is wrong with me?" or you could say to yourself that you're more suited for a better position. Something like, "I'm gonna focus on what is important in my life and the right job for me will come my way."

First things first, you really have to listen to yourself. When something happens or someone asks you to do something, pay close attention to your internal reaction. What is it that you are saying to yourself? Are you cheering yourself on, or are you saying, "I can't possibly do this"?

This shift is also about positive self-talk, along with reframing that internal conversation you're having with yourself. The goal is to be supportive, encouraging, and uplifting with yourself. Sometimes, you also need to look at the situation a little differently. Like I mentioned, you could look at the lost promotion as, "I'm not good enough," or you could look at it from the perspective of, "Oh, thank God I didn't get that job, because it wasn't the right one for me. There's a better one for me out there that fits my skill set and will help me to grow."

And funny thing is, this is where knowing your values, beliefs, what's important to you, and your purpose comes in handy, too. When you're rooted, you can use the aligning with your values and beliefs to help you reframe how you talk about an experience or situation. Accepting and appreciating what is good in our lives and living in that moment makes us feel more alive, more human. Life becomes more clear, with a whole new perspective and a grounded presence, allowing us to bend and flow with what comes our way in complete contentment and joy. I know this may sound too big-picture, but this is how you live a stress-free, healthy life—a life in gratitude and abundance. As an example, if you continue to look at being healthy as a challenge that's too time-consuming, exhausting, and unattainable, then you will never change or get out of the place you are in right now. However, if you look at being healthy as requiring just a few simple changes to your already daily routine to help you feel young again—alive in your own skin, living a vibrant life—then you're bound to change and find ways to improve your life. Change your mind and you can change your world!

It takes being present and being really in the situation to be able to shift perspective, but it also takes time to learn and build that skill. Don't shame yourself or beat yourself up for not getting it right on the first take. Start with one thing at a time. The next time you have a negative thought, listen to it and then flip that perspective around so you can take a more positive viewpoint and see what happens.

My life has been gnarly, dude. Twists and turns, challenging and occasionally frightening, but in retrospect it's been pretty amazing. That is definitely the most positive way I can look at my life.

Use the prompts below to help you shift to a more positive perspective on life:

• Take a moment and write down a list of negative thoughts, and then in the second column reframe each into a positive thought
• Complete one random act of kindness for someone this week
• Plan a lunch with your most positive friends, and enjoy the vibration that you can create together
• Try the 10-minute Loving-Kindness meditation via the Insight Timer app or your favorite meditation app. Or type this link into your browser: https://www.youtube.com/watch?v=auS1HtAz6Bs

Psych

/sĭk/
verb

1. used mockingly or playfully to indicate that one was joking or playing a prank: to trick someone.
Ex. "The future is already decided – Psych!"

(understanding mindfulness)

How many times in your life have you felt like the universe or God was saying, "Psych!"? Like you'd been on autopilot and all the sudden woken up to find that life was just happening to you and you had no idea what had been going on around you. It's almost like someone was just messing with you.

If you're anything like me, you've spent too much time focusing on the future, while clinging to the past, but never really being completely present. This never became more true than when I was at my very last corporate job—Let's call it "the hustle." There was a time when I was hustlin' that I didn't even eat lunch most days, and when I did, I wolfed it down in front of my computer and kept on going. Don't even get me started on how dehydrated, overweight, stressed, anxious, exhausted, and always sick or injured I was. I wore my multi-tasking maven identity like a badge of honor. As you know, we Gen-X women were taught that the multitasker is the one who wins.

We've praised ourselves and each other for managing all the things and thinking about everything and everyone all at once. Go ahead, give yourself a pat on the back and say, "Good on you, you super achieving lady boss." Now, back to my story.

I was managing a team of six other hustlers who were all working the same way—fried and tied to their computers for 12 hours a day on average. I was leading by example and living the kill-yourself-or-be-killed corporate culture. I had no grip on reality, no social life, no time for anything, and always told myself that once I hit this goal or once I got recognized or as soon as I get that promotion, I would be able to finally step foot in the corporate gym or take time for lunch with a friend. It was always someday soon I'll get to relax, slow down, take care of myself, and really live.

Obviously, that wasn't the healthiest lifestyle. I mean, I was stressed to the gills with all the side effects, but the biggest thing I was doing was letting life pass me by. Eventually, I had to take a pause and think about how I could enjoy a calm delicious lunch with friends each day, instead of living the way I was living. Like Ferris Bueller says, "Life moves pretty fast. If you don't stop and look around once in a while, you could miss it!"

When I finally snapped out of it and decided I wanted a better life, I began to think about what was wrong with how I was living and how I could improve it. I found out that multi-tasking is actually among the worst things you can do to your brain and body. It is stress incarnate and ultimately leads to burnout. It all makes sense when you think about how we try to live up to such a crazy and unrealistic standard of living, while still being expected to function at an optimal level. It goes without saying that I stopped multi-tasking immediately. I also began to research the art of mindfulness for reducing my stress.

Mindfulness is rooted deeply in the practice of meditation, which originated centuries ago in Hinduism and Buddhism as a way of approaching life in an enlightened state by being present. Lucky for us, it has now become an entire movement and an integral part of a healthy lifestyle.

Mindfulness is such a buzzword these days, but this hyper-aware way of paying attention to our present moment helps us to notice everything around us and in us. You can learn mindfulness techniques, practices, and skills for just about any purpose, but at its core it is the art of paying attention and being present. The goal is to be completely aware in the moment, like a child with no concept of past or concern for the future because it's just too big to comprehend.

Let me break it down in a way that's a little easier and more relevant to where you may be at this very moment. You know when you're lying there at night, as all women do, and you can't stop thinking to yourself, "I really need to get to sleep, oh my gosh is this a hot flash coming on? What am I going to make for dinner tomorrow night, are the kids okay, did I turn off the stove, did I ever call my mom back today?" Mindfulness is what can quickly ground you, your energy, so your brain can stop running on overdrive. It also helps you focus, think clearly, and root yourself in the present moment. Mindfulness is a simple regulation to help us feel safe, secure, and calm. It relieves stress, anxiety and depression. Mindfulness improves cognitive ability and slows the aging of the brain. It aids in pain management. If that isn't enough, it increases longevity and leads to a better quality of life through higher consciousness.

I started practicing meditation and energy work in my twenties and thirties, but I didn't find an intense need for it until years later when I was diagnosed with severe burnout. It was at that point in my life when I had to learn how to incorporate mindfulness techniques into my day to day routine. Through this need and much research, I learned you can incorporate mindfulness into everything you do. As an example, when Travis and I began our initial health journey, we started with mindful eating. For this practice, we had to slow down and intentionally set ourselves up for success. This meant we would sit at the table, like adults, instead of eating in front of the television. We had to think more about the digestive process. We learned that if you scarf your food down, you aren't actually allowing your body enough time to fully engage the digestive process. The more you chew the more time you allow saliva to develop, which aids in the breakdown of the food in the gut. It became a common practice for us to count each time we chewed a bite of food. It also was important for us to pause and drink water, allowing our bodies time to actually feel our fullness. It's not often we, humans, take a moment while having a meal to think about if we're full, if we need another bite, or if we have to finish what is on the plate. The moment we did this, we were practicing mindfulness without really realizing that is what we were doing. We became more present. We even began to listen to our bodies and take a 20-minute break once we were 80% full, so we could fully understand if we were full or needed more food. It sounds like a lot, but we actually began to be able to hear our bodies and built up the ability to know when we were and were not hungry, which in turn helped us know when to stop eating. By mindfully eating, we gave our body more time to properly digest our meals, which improved our digestive systems and helped us repair our gut microbiome. It was a total win-win! Eating this way and sharing some of the techniques we mastered, we became examples for our son (who we called the food cobra), our family, and our friends.

For me, mindfulness is a moment to be still and to listen to yourself and process your gut instincts with an intense hyper-awareness. Over the years, I've practiced yoga, mantra, loving kindness, spiritual, body scan, chakra, guided, mindfulness, and visualization meditation, breathwork, and Reiki energy work, incorporating different styles and teachings into what is now my mindfulness practice. I've come to the realization that there are no wrong ways to be present. Whatever technique or practice you choose to use, you should always make sure it is one that suits you and aligns with your spiritual values and beliefs. While I like a guided meditation, gratitude practice, or binaural beats, my husband practices Transcendental Meditation (TM) 20 minutes twice a day to get regulated and grounded to each new day. We both do it differently, and that is great because at least we're doing it.

If I can be completely honest, it wasn't until I got fully aware of how I was living that I really began to live mindfully, in the present, grounded in each moment. It was then that life started to feel on track.

By now you may be asking yourself, where can I get some of that magic?

Breathing is a good place to start. It's the one thing that will bring you right into the moment without even having to think about it. If you're connected to your breath and concentrating on your breath, you can't not be present. If you've ever taken a yoga class, you'll understand how important your breath can be to remaining in the moment. The one thing you concentrate on while practicing yoga is being conscious of your breath and how you're breathing. The goal is to have deep diaphragmatic breaths, so your whole body will be breathing. If you lose your center and start to get caught up in all your swirling thoughts again, you are getting out of the now. The one thing your yogi will tell you is to go back to your breath, concentrate on your breath. It is the one thing that will calm your mind and get you present again. What's amazing is that you're also regulating your nervous system, lowering your heart rate, balancing your stress hormones, slowing down your racing mind, and even managing your menopausal symptoms. Who wouldn't want that? So just breathe.

The practice of yoga itself is also a very mindful practice. Years ago, when I started my yoga journey (I'm talking the 90s, ladies), I saw an interview with Russell Simmons. Yes, that Russell Simmons. Def Jam Records. I caught an interview once where he was talking about how he had found yoga and had taught himself to always practice with a smile on his face. I found this fascinating because I had never thought about anything other than trying to calm my face or relax. Keeping a smile on my face while I practiced was a completely novel idea. He recommended smiling when practicing difficult poses, working with your body to breathe into and find the happiness within each pose, smile, and breath. He was captivated by yoga Asana Practice being the science of happiness and went on to share that he felt we should smile and breathe even when we encounter difficulties off the mat. Such a beautiful synergy, how a simple mindfulness practice like yoga can carry over to a more mindful approach to your day to day experiences.

Another mindful technique I love to do is what I call the rag doll. This is a fun full body relaxation that forces you to experience and connect with every muscle in your body from the crown of your head to the tip of each toe. You start by either sitting in a comfortable seated position in a chair or on the floor, or you could actually just lie down. Then starting at the crown of your head, you fully relax every part of your body as you move down. Relax your head and your eyes, your temples, your jaw. Let go. Continue down the entire body, your chest, and your shoulders, letting everything drop and droop. Just like with a rag doll, if someone were to pick you up, every part of you would just slump. This exercise is fun when you get to the fingers and toes because most of us don't even think about feeling our little extremities let alone relaxing them. As you relax your neck, stomach and back, you may begin to slump over if you're sitting. Be careful not to fall over, but go with it if you can. Once you get to full connectedness and relaxation, then you want to slowly begin to bring life back into your body by wiggling your fingers and toes. Then begin to feel more strength taking hold and slowly, if seated, rolling back up into your seated posture. Flutter your eyes open and sit in that state of being for one more moment before you give yourself back to the world.

Hmm, I'm relaxed and really present just writing this for you.

The last technique I want to leave you with is something to help you engage with the space around you and within you. This is something I learned when studying positive psychology and may be easier to do when you don't have the time for a full-body relaxation, like when you're at the office. Whether you're in the office or at home, you can engage all five of your senses to help you become more present. You can do this practice with your eyes open or closed, but you first want to start with what you can see. Think about or look around the space you are in and check out some detail that you wouldn't normally notice at first glance. The easiest would be a shadow. You want to identify five new and interesting things you can see in that space. Next, become aware of four things you can feel. It might be the smooth buttons on your computer keyboard or the air blowing against your skin. Then, concentrate on three sounds you can hear. If you are in the office, you might hear the sound of the computer fan. Now, notice two things you can smell. Maybe you're walking in a park and can smell the dampness of the undergrowth or the perfume of the person you just walked past. Finally, focus on something you can taste, so take a drink of your coffee or taste the salt air. Simply engaging your senses can connect you to the present, grounding you and providing you with an enhanced awareness of where you are in this moment and time.

Being connected to the present moment can put you into a completely different state of mind. It's noticing the little details of life that calm us and bring us back to present reality. These are just a few ideas of how to practice mindfulness. There are new techniques and opportunities to explore with practicing mindfulness from forest bathing to painting, journaling to exercise. Whatever you choose to do to get yourself in the moment, enjoy it with all your heart, let go of your stress, and reprogram yourself to experience life and all its delicious moments, so it doesn't pass you by.

Here are a couple of prompts to get you headed in a more mindful direction:

• Have dinner at the table one night this week and take your time to enjoy every bite
• During your next office meeting, stop and relax your forehead and smile
• Grab a pencil and a piece of paper and draw the room where you're sitting
• Take a nature walk and use your five senses to ground yourself in the moment

Homegirl

/hohm-gurl/
noun

1. a girl or woman from one's neighborhood, hometown, or region. broadly: a female friend. a member of one's peer group.
Ex. *"My homegirl can always read my mind."*

(creating deep connections)

Where would we be without our "homegirls"? Having deep lasting relationships with positive forces for good elevates everyone's health and wellness in ways we've never thought possible. Even the longest lived people on the planet attribute it to their reason for longer, better quality of life. You need friends to feed your life. I honestly can't imagine a life without friends and a strong tribe of women to carry me through.

Let's begin our friend journey by considering when we're young. I remember it being so easy to make friends when I was young. You didn't even have to think about it. It was as easy as, "You like Play-Doh? I like Play-Doh. Let's make things out of Play-Doh together." How could it be hard with every one of us being dropped off to spend hours in one room or a central classroom for hours on end to play, nap, hang out, and just be ourselves together? We were our young, authentic selves. The beauty of it was that we were naturally, dare I say energetically, drawn to each other—positive attracting to positive. We were too young to be in a negative head space, except that one kid that bit everyone (you know who I'm talking about). Everybody was about having as much fun as possible, getting other people involved, and getting the most out of the daylight, on and off the playground.

Fast forward to middle school and let the games begin. This is where we began to struggle to keep old friends and make new ones. This phase was where we all had to work to be accepted. Tough when you're encountering all of society's expectations around beauty, along with trying to be cool or in the cool group. Ugh, I was so awkward at this stage in my life. I had to get glasses in third grade, which was completely devastating. Add to that the hairstyle of the time was to have your hair feathered. If you didn't know, you cannot feather curly hair unless you frizz it out. Guess what happened? I was a frizzed-out mess with glasses. Oh yeah, and did I mention that I decided to frost my hair too?!?!? When I tell you I was awkward, I'm not lying. Everybody was wearing Jordache jeans and Camp Beverly Hills, while I was in my Sassons and a hand-me-down crushed velvet sweater. I did manage to save up my babysitting money for a couple of shirts from Pasta, an offshoot of Paul Harris (both of which closed in 1991). Anyway, you get the gist—I was anything but cool to anyone except my immediate friends and family.

This is when I first started to experience mean girls. Our mean girls were nothing like Regina George. I'm talking straight-up *Heathers*, like when Veronica says, "She's my best friend. God, I hate her."[17] I can still feel the pure yuck and anxiety creep up my back just thinking about it, but I made it through pretty unscathed. I managed to work high school like a buffet with a friend from each different clique. From stoners to nerds, popular girls to theater chicks, athletes to artists, I had them all covered. If I had to put myself in a bucket, I would have been the art school girl. I was actually voted "Most Artistic Girl" by my senior classmates—such an honor.

Unlike most girls of our generation who have held tight to the tribe they developed in high school, I went on to develop different relationships in college and beyond. At this point in my life, when I would say that I'm at my most authentic, I have a close handful of friends whom I've held on to from various stages of my life. These are the ones who have outlasted my ups and downs and loved me anyway. These have been some of my most valuable and long lasting relationships to date.

So why are friendships so important?

There's a science behind friendships. They keep us living longer, but only when they are deep quality friendships with positive people. Those types of friendships enrich our lives and improve our health and wellness. Those deep, social connections have significant health implications, both mentally and physically. They provide us with a sense of belonging and acceptance, supporting us emotionally, but they also help us reduce our stress, boost our self-esteem, reduce feelings of depression, lower our blood pressure, and even help us maintain a healthy weight.

Don't get me started on the power of laughter with a friend for boosting moods, fighting stress, strengthening your immune system, and giving you all the positive vibes you can handle. Those strong experiences and emotions can do wonders for the soul, as well as our minds and bodies, helping us to become better people.

When we surround ourselves with people who support us unconditionally, with love in their hearts and positive attitudes, we thrive.

No, I'm not talking about superficial friendships here, like surface friendships. You know, the friendship you have with a peer or acquaintance you see in passing at a networking event, where you're cordial and familiar, but really don't know them on a deeply personal level. I'm talking about deep-level friendships with women who respect, love, and support you no matter what the circumstance. Those friends—you know the ones—that you could be miles away from, but they would pick up the phone or hop on a plane in a heartbeat if you needed them. The ones who will tell you the ultimate truth whether you want to hear it or not, but with love in their hearts. These are real friends.

I absolutely love the opening lyrics to the *Friends* theme song[18] to explain what I mean by a real friend.

So no one told you life was gonna be this way
Your job's a joke, you're broke
Your love life's DOA
It's like you're always stuck in second gear
When it hasn't been your day, your week, your month
Or even your year, but
I'll be there for you
(When the rain starts to pour)
I'll be there for you
(Like I've been there before)
I'll be there for you
('Cause you're there for me too)

We've talked before about creating this group of real friends, a support system of positive women. It was the basis for one of the keys to combating stress in Chapter 2, but now you know just how important having homegirls can be to your life. It is imperative that you have a group of women who support you in different ways. You need the mentor, the listener, the comedian, the cheerleader, the one with all the ideas, the truth teller, and the one who will cut a bitch. Some of these may be the same person, because some people are great at more than one role. You probably will find that your friends cross over into different roles at different times in your life, but it's important to find someone or more than one person in your life that can give you these types of support. It's okay if you're struggling to think of who in your life who would fit into each of those categories. You may be missing someone for one, two, or more; but fear not, you can make new friends even as an adult.

So what do we do to make friends as adults?

Building rapport is one thing, but relationships take time. For this we need to come up with some fun ways we can make—and, more importantly, keep—friends in our midlife and beyond. Let's face it, making friends at this age is more difficult than when we were children. We have had a full life, rich with experiences, so as adults we tend to be cautious around new people--and sometimes maybe not cautious enough. For this very reason, most of us will get up in our head about meeting and spending time with new people, making it more difficult than it needs to be. So this is why making friends is easier when we're doing something fun, creative, or enjoyable.

The trick is to find people that you have common ground with, people that maybe have similar interests, are in a similar industry, or like to do the same things. These are your low-hanging-fruit friendship pools. In order to find these people, you've gotta actually put yourself out there. This may entail spending time at industry events or conferences, going to group activities for hobbies you enjoy, joining a workout class, attending a networking event, or even popping into a quick yoga session at the beach. Whatever it is you choose to embrace, you have to be active and actively looking for new friends. It's like being a kid again. Put yourself into a space with people your own age that have similar interests and childlike state, so you can ask someone if they like Play-Doh. If you're doing something fun and playful, that keeps you active and engaged with others, you're gonna naturally make connections with people. It's those connections that are sometimes the beginning of what could be an incredible friendship.

Think about joining a walking club, taking a cooking class, learning how to paint, volunteer for a charity close to your heart, become a member of a book club, request a membership to a local women's organization on Facebook, attend an event hosted by the local chamber of commerce, sign up for a retreat or conference, or get on Eventbrite and subscribe to local events, so you know what's going on in your area. Remember to make sure that you're doing something that you find fun and will put you in the mix with people also having fun.

When I moved to my current home, I knew nobody in town or even in this part of the country. I had to set out to make new friends. After all, you can't live somewhere and not have that friend you can go to dinner with or shift shopping on a Saturday together. I remember being at one of the first networking events I attended and having a woman ask me what I wanted to get out of that evening. I was taken aback, but with a straight face I looked at her and said, "I'm just here to make friends." Now, my response totally turned her off, and that was fine by me because she wasn't one of my people. However, I did make a similar statement to other people the same night with whom I'm now developing friendships, so you just never know. I will say that honesty is the best policy; and if what you're looking for is a new friend, it's okay to just tell someone that very thing.

This may be a scary concept for some of you who aren't type-A extroverts. You don't have to smile, shake a hand, and say, "be my friend," but you might have to put yourself out there from time to time and sometimes be the one to talk first. For example, picture yourself in an art class. You're sitting at your easel painting away and right next to you is another new artist. You could sit there quietly and paint, or you could make a new friend by being the one to strike up a conversation. It can be as easy as saying hi, or it might be more interesting if you ask your neighbor some questions like, "Is this your first art class?" or "That looks great. Is that painting of a place you go on vacation?" Whatever happens, you must be prepared to be the one to make the first move. I did this very thing at a yoga retreat I attended a couple years ago. I sat right down next to someone, said hi, and struck up a conversation. It wasn't easy. I had to muster up courage to do that, but once I got to asking my neighbor questions, it wasn't long before we were planning to try out a local yoga studio together for a new class someone had told her about. This didn't evolve into a lasting friendship, but that led to me meeting someone else, which led to me meeting another gal; and that led me to an open house event where I met a now dear friend. A new ride-or-die that I would have never met if I hadn't put myself out there in the first place.Don't forget to keep connected with the friends you've already cultivated. Since moving away from most of my longtime friends, I have struggled with staying in touch with everyone. While some of these friendships will fade away, the strong lasting friendships will remain with little effort. As we get older, it seems we only get busier with commitments and family, so it becomes imperative that we make time to connect with those we treasure. Now, sometimes you can go for months without talking to somebody, and when you see them again it's just like you've been sitting right next to them all along, but that takes a special kind of friend and friendship. I have a friend with whom I can always pick up just where we left off, even after years. But when we get off the phone, I always wonder why I waited so long to reach out because I adore her so much. That's a true friend. Then again, so are the ones I talk to every other day. You have to know who your friend is and what type of communicator they are. It's a mutual agreement of sorts when you decide on the cadence of your communications. It's whatever works for you both.

Sometimes friendships can take a pause, and then you can pick up decades later, reconnect, and chat away. And sometimes you can't. I have a few thoughts and stories about this to share.

I believe that people come in and out of your life at different times and for different reasons. I've had the pleasure of having had a life filled with an over abundance of friends, all amazing and necessary for the moment and time of my life that they were a part of. Several of these friendships have faded away for good reason. We've been on different paths; our lives no longer need to coexist; something negative has happened that broke the friendship; and other times we just forgot about each other. Each of those situations has happened when and exactly at the moment it needed to be over. If you take an inventory of your life, you may have experienced a similar situation.

The laws of attraction are also at play. Positive attracts positive, and negative bounces off and away. You may notice, as you become more true to yourself and authentic, that negative people and influences in your life will bounce away. The trick is to know when it's time to let them go. This is where you need to listen to your gut instincts and act on them. If you're really listening to yourself, more often than not, you'll know the difference between a friendship that is nourishing and one that is toxic or has run its course. The strength is in being honest with yourself and them and letting it go. It often can feel like a breakup, but believe me, it will be the best thing for you and your growing and changing life.

To be honest, I've had five such friendships. I'm glad I can only count them on one hand, because they were the hardest friendships to walk away from. I won't relive them here, but I will say that at the time I realized they weren't the friendships for me, I was at major turning points in my life. I was changing dramatically, becoming more myself and growing up and out of the life I was living. They were such transformations that I had a couple of these friends tell me they didn't know who I was and that they wanted the old me back. Seriously, they both said this, and they were friendships I had cultivated decades apart from one another. It makes sense because when I grow, I grow quickly, and it's pretty unforgiving with regards to my old self. My hope is that my sharing this means you won't have to go through anything near as dramatic as I've experienced, but I know it's out of my hands. I wish you good friend fortune.

On a lighter note, I have reconnected with a couple good friends who have come in and out of my life. Nothing has been lasting, but it was great to catch up and share a coffee and a few laughs over old times. Never hesitate to rekindle or reconnect with those you still think about now and then. You never know how they may turn out.

Friendships are vital to our health and well-being, but it takes finding your people - those you gel with on a spiritual, emotional, and mental level - to make having a friend worthwhile. Remember, a friendship isn't the place to lose yourself and conform, it is a place to be your true authentic self, to listen, commiserate, celebrate, provide honest perspective, love, laugh, and live to the fullest. Better yet, think of it this way... We need to find those women with whom we can completely take our mask off, those who you could ugly cry in front of as you down an entire bowl of queso yourself with no regrets, those who will cheer you on as you lip sync and dance to Sir Mix-A-Lot's "Big Butts" in your living room, those who always want you to win. That's a friendship worth hanging onto for dear (mid-) life.

Before you move on, here are a few prompts to help you get started on creating deeper connections:

• Choose one friend, call her tonight, and tell her you miss her.
• Grab a group of friends together, old and new, and go do something fun—try a paint class, a wellness triathlon, or just a long ladies brunch.
• Make a point to introduce yourself to someone new this week or at least just say hello.
• The next time a friend calls with news, ask her how you can support, what she needs. This will set you up for a more mindful conversation and help your friend get exactly what she needs.

Crib

/krib/
noun

2. an apartment or house.
Ex. *"Your crib is so warm and inviting."*

(grounding in a healthy home)

How much did you love watching MTV *Cribs*? Seeing how our Gen-X music icons lived was like peering into a fantasy world. It was almost as good as *Lifestyles of the Rich and Famous*. I was fascinated with people's homes then and now. From playing with Fisher-Price Little People and their house to *Cribs*, every bit of my childhood sparked a lasting love of architecture and design.

I grew up in a family who did this to the fullest extent. My mother was constantly rearranging the furniture, changing rooms around, painting the walls new colors or wallpapering everything, changing styles, refreshing the look to fit the season, and in some cases going with a whole new theme (you gotta love the 80s). My family loved new spaces; in fact, we counted it up recently and my mother has actually lived in 9 homes in my hometown. Seriously, it's a thing. All of this is to say that my interest in this comes naturally.

To say I'm obsessed is a bit much, but my passion for interior and exterior design runs deep. If I want to calm my mind and turn on the creative juices, I just walk through a hardware store, tile shop, art store, or furniture showroom—or the Holy Grail that is the architectural salvage store. It's such a part of my soul. My authentic self craves creating with my hands and is focused on transforming spaces for mindful living, harmony, and a greater quality of life.

Why am I going on about this? Well, it's because I know how important the built environment has become over the years and now more than ever, since we're spending more and more time indoors.

Let's go back to the beginning, to get a better look at why we should even care. One of the basic human needs for survival is shelter. That's all well and good for the caveman, but we've evolved to see our home as so much more. It's become a place of refuge, safety, sanctuary, retreat, respite, and escape. We use it as a place to hang out with people we love, celebrate life's big moments, and escape from the big bad world. It has even become a reflection of who we are and can enhance our lives. This is where the wellness aspect comes into play.

The World Health Organization (WHO) has designated our environment as one of the social determinants of health. At the core, your immediate environment has a major effect on your quality of life and your health. After all, on average Americans spend 90% of our total lifetime indoors. The health impact is bigger than just the built structure. It is about the toxicity of materials used, the location, and the proximity to resources that help improve your life. When all these areas align to support a healthy lifestyle, we call this "environmental wellness."

Usually, environmental wellness becomes an area of concern when there are noticeable inequalities that are affecting the health of a group of people. I'm sure you've heard of the term "food desert." Living in a food desert means that you don't have access to a grocery store where you can buy fresh food. This lack of access directly affects a person's health. This is an example of how our environment plays such an important role in our well-being. However, the facets of this wellness dimension range from the built environment to the community you live in and the larger natural ecosystem and biosphere. For our purposes, we're going to focus on one simple, yet basic building block you can explore right now to improve your quality of life.

As I've stated, environment plays a very important role in your well-being. When we live in a space that is pleasant and stimulating, it can support our health, reconnect us to ourselves and nature, and improve all dimensions of well-being.

Think about the impact of something as simple as spring cleaning on your mood and your energy. It really shakes things up, not to mention shaking off the winter dust. Add to this a little seasonal decor, bright-colored flowers, fabrics and colors, and some fresh new plants, and you've created an instant place of enhanced wellness.

True health begins with your immediate domain. Improving environmental wellness is simple and results in a more harmonious lifestyle. This particular dimension of wellness encourages you to practice habits that promote a healthy environment, while respecting your natural surroundings. By doing so, you can increase your holistic health. Updating any space, be it home or office, will directly impact your state of mind, emotional well-being, physical health, and productivity. Your immediate space can support you in anything you want to achieve. When your home is designed for wellness, it will keep you grounded in healthy living.

We're all so obsessed with eating right, exercising, and improving our lifestyle to live longer and healthier, but we never stop to think how our mood, energy level, stress level, productivity, weight, high blood pressure, and sometimes chronic illness are directly impacted by our built environment. In all of my work in wellness, I have come to understand that the easiest and maybe the most important place to start when you want to get healthy is with your home. I know it sounds too good to be true, but think about it...

If you want to lose weight—How is your kitchen helping you make healthier choices?

If you want better sleep—How is your bedroom supporting greater rest?

If you want to manage your stress—How is your home calming you down?

Your space contributes to your health and happiness by reducing your stress, helping relieve anxiety, keeping you feeling safe and secure, lowering blood pressure, and providing you with clean air and water, to name a few. In fact, it makes such an impact that it's actually one of the dimensions of wellness. Your environmental health affects all other areas of your well-being, so it's no surprise that improving it can impact your mental, emotional, and physical health, enriching your quality of life.

One of the easiest ways to set yourself up for success, improve your life, and be your best self is to stop and take a look around your space. When you look around your home or office, do you get depressed, tired, or unmotivated? Are you having trouble sleeping? Do you find it tough to find a healthy snack in your kitchen? It just may be that your space is keeping you from living and being your best.

If you feel your space could better support the healthy life you want to live, you need to create an environment that supports well-being, emphasizes harmony and balance, connects you to nature, and increases your quality of life. It's bigger than the design; it's creating a feeling, a wellness experience. A good place to start is to consider how your home feels.

How does your home make you feel?

We have those connections to our homes, whether they are warm and cozy or clean and modern. No matter the feeling, we're all so pulled to our homes for multiple reasons. When it comes to setting up your environment for health, it really isn't about the style; it's more about the feeling. Your mental and emotional health are affected by your environment, and the feeling you desire can be set up in conjunction with any design style. You don't have to look like you're in a resort in Tulum to be living in a wellness space. You can still have this emotional response and stay true to your personal style.

Once you get clear on how your home makes you feel, you need to decide if that is good enough or not. In order to do this, you need to answer a series of questions.

• How does my home encourage a healthy lifestyle?

- How can my home provide me with greater mental and emotional comfort?
- Is my home welcoming?
- Does my space connect me to nature?
- Does it improve your physical health?
- What am I trying to achieve?

This last question is so very important, because just like having a vision for your health and what a healthy life looks like helps you focus on how to get there, having a clear picture of what you are trying to achieve will help you design a space to support that goal or habit.

As an example, I had a client who wanted to achieve a healthy body size for her shape. In order to do that, she set a weight loss and exercise goal. One of her goals was to cook healthier meals at home. When I asked her if her kitchen was set up to support her in eating and cooking healthy meals, she laughed out loud; but when she stopped, she had an aha moment. We talked about how important it was to set up her space for healthy eating and choices, and then we got busy. When we started in her space, we went directly to the pantry first. We emptied it and took a good long inventory of all the foods, separating them into categories of real versus processed food. After we had everything out and divided, we broke them down into categories of veggies, grains, pastas, sauces, on and on. Gradually we started building back her pantry, but this time with purpose. We strategically put all of the real food at eye level by category, intentionally grouping them as ingredients that would align with each other for a meal. This made it very simple for her to plan and "shop" her pantry for each meal. We didn't throw away any of the processed food. We followed suit and categorized it, placing them in the pantry on the top and bottom shelves. This placement was intentional, so that she would have to make a conscious choice to grab for them. We went on to reorganize her cabinets, countertops and refrigerator. We rearranged the space to add a smoothie bar, coffee and tea station, and a resting place for fresh grab-n-go fruits. We made it very easy for her to keep to her goals and make healthy choices daily.

She went on to design a space to support her exercise goal

of building strength, as well as a space in her home to practice meditation, gratitude, and spiritual growth. She was set up for success and her home supported her journey to her ideal size. Side note: She is happy and living lighter these days, stronger than ever.

My advice is to be very clear on your goals before you get to re-designing your space for wellness. Once you have this clarity, you can begin.

Where do I even begin?

I always begin at the beginning. How you feel when you enter your domain is so very important to the overall experience you have within your home and your life. From the entryway and throughout the entire home, you'll need to take an inventory.

An environmental inventory is a great place to start when setting yourself up for new behaviors. Walk throughout your home and go back to the questions we asked in the beginning to gain a better understanding of how you feel in each space, how you want to feel in the space, and what you need each space to do for you. I did this for my client before we started in on her kitchen, the same way I took an inventory of my own kitchen.

I wanted to eat healthier, plan my meals in advance, and incorporate smoothies into my daily plan. Therefore, I set up my pantry, so that the shelf at eye level contains all of the food I need for the week, including snacks. At the end of the week, I replenish this shelf with new food for my upcoming meal plan. The shelf below has cookbooks and bulk items like oatmeal, chia seeds, nuts, and breadcrumbs, with a variety of flours, adaptogenics, and teas to replenish as needed. I keep my spices and cooking utensils in the cabinets right by my stove for easy access when cooking. Hanging on the side of the fridge is the meal plan for the current week. Of course, I also have all the equipment and tools I need to cook healthy meals daily, stored where they will be easy to access. I've intentionally designed my space to help keep me on track to eat healthy every day.

This exercise of taking an environmental inventory isn't limited to the kitchen. You can apply this to any space in your home, office, or anywhere you spend a length of time. This might sound like an exercise in crazy, but hear me out. This is a great place to start when setting yourself up for new behaviors. Beyond the space planning, you'll also want to take an inventory of the other small details. Lighting, colors, smells, and even the patterns or textures on your furnishings will impact your health.

You may not realize it, but these simple changes can help you reduce anxiety, improve your immune function, lower stress, enhance sleep quality, and so much more.

Wellness Design incorporates elements like natural light, biophilic furniture, living plants, rich textures, curated colors, and organic materials into mindful spaces carefully curated to support a healthy lifestyle. The idea is not to just give your home's interior a refresh. It's to create a space that is the embodiment of wellness, supportive of your health and a place that enables you to improve your life. You'll end up with spaces that not only exude aesthetic brilliance but also foster a sense of tranquility, harmony, and health. It would be impossible to teach you everything you would need to know about designing to wellness in one chapter of this book, so I'm going to give you a few things to think about that will allow you to imagine how you might enhance your own space.

The easiest place for you to begin is by using your five senses. Your senses of touch, taste, smell, sight, and hearing can help you determine what is needed within any space so that you can improve it for greater well-being. These simple things can make a big impact.

Taste

We've discussed the food element already, so I won't explore it much more. The kitchen is all about taste, so setting up easy ways to interact with healthy foods is necessary. Try adding a bowl of fruit on the counter or dining room table. Maybe even keep a nut dish in the living room for people who come over to enjoy. I always keep ginger chews or honey sticks in my office for a quick afternoon pick-me-up. Think about how you can add taste into your space.

Sight

There is nothing more disturbing to the female human experience within a space than seeing clutter. The visual appearance of clutter can induce anxiety, depression, tension, and for all you peri-menopausal women, irritability. You'll actually have a physical reaction in response to clutter. Chaos creates chaos, so a quick declutter can lower anxiety and inadvertent stress, but it can also give you greater mental clarity. Lose the clutter quick, and use the same rule for your home as you would for your closet. If you haven't used it in a year, you may not need it.

After you clear the clutter, give your space a deep clean. We've talked about this before, but a deep cleaning feels so good. It revitalizes your mood, boosts your energy, calms you down, leaves you feeling safe and secure, and even helps you feel more in control.

Another easy-to-see design change is in your lighting. While it's always good to have as much natural light as possible throughout a space, it is important to have the proper lighting for the task at hand. Reading lights, kitchen task lighting, and evenings by candlelight are examples of how lighting has a specific purpose that dictates its form and function. One thing that is good to know when selecting bulbs for your fixtures, try to use analog (incandescent) bulbs to lessen your exposure to the blue light associated with LED bulbs. While LED lights are good for the environment, the blue light they produce disrupts your sleep by slowing the secretion of melatonin, altering your circadian rhythm. In some cases of prolonged exposure, it can also cause major damage to the eye, leading to chronic eye issues like, macular degeneration.

Have you ever wondered why people ask you if you have a favorite color? Color plays an important role in our everyday lives. Our feelings, personalities, memories, actions, and even dreams are associated with color. Color plays a major role in improving our health and well-being. It's true, our mental, physical, spiritual, and emotional health can be enhanced or flip side, wrecked by color. A pop of color can change your mood, raise your blood pressure, increase your metabolism, make you feel calm, strain your eyes, energize you, and even make you happy. Because color creates emotional and sometimes physical responses, it's important to consider colors carefully when designing your space. Before you add color, you need to be clear on how you want people to feel when they walk into the room, the mood you want to create, and what color makes you feel good. Our reactions and emotional responses are very personal, so be very selective when using color in your home. Color is a very personal experience, so make sure you check in with yourself when deciding to decorate with color.

Pro Tip: If you're trying to lose weight, eat from a blue plate. Blue is the most unappetizing color and will subconsciously make you eat less.

Smell

The right scent can provoke intense emotions and happiness. Smells are unique and can evoke emotional responses, memories, improved energy levels, and more. Setting your space up with a scent that makes you feel good or puts you in the right frame of mind is an important part of wellness design. Add a scent that you like, based on what you want to feel in the room or space. Think about scents that give you energy, relax you, help you focus, make you smile, or feel like a warm hug. Once you determine what smell you need, try adding it to your office or home. You can use an oil in a diffuser, soy candle, or flowering plant to bring your favorite scent inside. Don't forget to take a moment and notice how your day changes.

Touch

Our sense of touch is a key factor in human survival and your health, yet it really is one of those senses we take for granted. From the day you are born, touch is used to calm you both emotionally and physically. It helps you feel safe and loved, reduces your heart rate, lowers your stress levels, helps you bond with other people, and provides pleasure. It's no wonder that working with your hands makes you feel so good. Japanese, Italian, and Greek cultures (among others) teach gardening and working with your hands as a key to longevity. Now, think about this in your home.

Any designer will tell you that texture creates visual dimension in any space. However, it's the sensory experience of natural elements like wood, stone, or natural textiles (soft and rough) that creates a sense of balance and harmony. The goal when designing for wellness is to create a tactile experience that makes you feel good. You can create comfort and a sense of relaxation by adding fluffy blankets, soft pillows, or plush rugs. Wood elements, natural rugs like jute, or live plants create a sense of security, warmth, calm, connection, and life. Adding texture to your space provides a sense of calm, groundedness, tranquility, harmony, and even intimacy. This is the perfect moment to add a little texture to your life.

Sound

There truly is nothing like sitting down for a moment with a warm cup of tea to relax and enjoy the inviting glow and sound of a crackling fire. For me, the sound of a crackling fire sparks joy and happiness, but what you may not know is that a sound like this can enhance your overall health. Natural sounds and music can reduce stress, improve mood, lower blood pressure, soothe pain, increase energy levels, decrease risk of chronic illness, and so much more. However, there are also sounds that can do the exact opposite.

I love a good impromptu dance party in the kitchen with a great '80s mix of TLC, Whitney Houston, Prince, and let's not forget 2LiveCrew. On the flip side, I also love to rest and sleep to binaural beats. Choosing the right sounds for a space is an important endeavor, so take your time.

I hope this gets you started in creating a crib you'll want to come home to. Small adjustments like these can create an atmosphere and an experience which improves your well-being-—helping you relax, uplift your spirits, and nurture relationships all just by making improvements to your interior environment. Make sure to create a space that matches your style and soothes your soul. You'll be amazed at the difference a few changes to your space can make to your well-being. One thing I can guarantee is that healthy starts at home.

One more thing, here are a few prompts to
help you create a space for wellness:

• Add a small pop of color to your office or favorite
space. Think vase, coffee mug, pillow, framed
painting, etc.
• Find a sound or song that energizes you and
throw an impromptu dance party in your kitchen,
while you make dinner.
• Clean up your indoor air quality by adding a
snake plant or aloe vera plant——-time for some
pure air (thanks, plants).
• Make your own room spray by filling a small
2-ounce spray bottle ¾ full with witch hazel and
12 drops of your favorite essential oil.

Phat

/fat/
adjective

1. fashionable, stylish.
Ex. *"This dress is phat."*
2. highly attractive or gratifying: Excellent.
Ex. *"There's a phat beat moving through my body."*

(the illusive self-image)

As Gen-X women, we've lived through ALL the diet culture craze and madness. No wonder we're all obsessed about our body weight, shape, and size. Not a one of us came out unscathed by what we lived through, but this doesn't have to define us or hold us back. It's time we love ourselves. Instead of seeing ourselves as FAT, we should see ourselves PHAT.

In a recent conversation with my mother, I broached the topic of body positivity and the body dysmorphia created by societal standards. We unearthed a generational trauma worth exploring. Our mothers were raised to become wives. They were nurtured toward college not to get a degree, but to get their MRS. Can you believe they actually used that statement? Anyway, if you think about how normal that was and the importance put on looks as a way to attract a husband, it's amazing we turned out as well as we did. We were given more opportunities but we still received a heavy dose of obsession over how we look.

Having studied art in high school and college, I spent a lot of my time studying the body and the changing shapes throughout art history. A robust, shapely woman has been considered beautiful and revered for centuries. You can see the representations in the works of the masters and to this day those standards are used as reference in modern culture. For instance, Robert Downey Jr.'s character Jack in The Pick-Up Artist says, "Did anyone ever tell you that you have the face of a Botticelli and the body of a Degas?"[19] as he tries to pick up Molly Ringwald's character, Randy. I'm sure you've also heard of the Rubenesque figure a time or two in reference to a full-figured woman. It wasn't until the invention of the camera that we changed our idea of the ideal female form and turned to waif-like models such as Twiggy to set a new standard of beauty.

Why do we even care?

We care because we're human. Humans have an innate need to belong at all costs. Being isolated or worse excluded is detrimental to our well-being. Because of this fundamental need, we start trying to conform and fit in from an early age. Like it or not, your looks are what is important to being liked because that is what is valued in our society.

Our need to be liked is also how we form our own self-image. As we grow, we have experiences in life that help us form beliefs about ourselves, but when we read, see, and hear what society says will make people like us, we alter our self-image. These thoughts become ingrained in our minds and begin to twist those beliefs in different directions. The more negative your self-image becomes, the more likely you are to develop anxiety, depression, eating disorders, body dysmorphia, stress, and so much more.

Sounds horrifying when you lay all that truth out there like this, but it's helpful in understanding why our self-image may or may not be somewhat distorted from trying to fit in for so long. I love what a friend of mine said about it all: "There's work to be done, but we've been brainwashed and now have brain fog."

How you see, feel, and respect yourself permeates out into the world and shows up when you engage with others. If you think negatively about yourself, you tend to give off a negative vibe and a negative energy that brings everything down. The opposite is true when you feel positive and good about yourself. You can boost everyone's mental and emotional physical well-being with the positive energy you create when you have confidence.

We've been so conditioned and warped by society regarding our personal appearance. Quite frankly, this does a real number on our self-image, body and all. The shame, guilt, and anxiety of my formative years was a real deal. I remember looking in the mirror and picking myself apart. If you remember the "pinch an inch" message, then you share my mirror experience. I would measure my thinness on the pinch method. I cringe today for that young girl and her warped sense of self.

I recently went through a pile of photos from high school as I was trying to purge my collection of memorabilia. Junior year, I thought my body was way too big and I remember being on a diet to get smaller. Nobody even questioned my eating habits or had a conversation with me about how ridiculous that was, but when I found the picture of my 110-pound form, I about died. I literally gasped out loud. I'm actually sad for her that she thought she was fat and needed a diet. I looked good and in no way did I need to worry about my size, but because of the '80s idea of pretty, I was affected. I would honestly give anything for that body today. True confessions... I stand in the mirror today, hold my arm up, shake it, and watch the extra arm fat jiggle in amazement. Less judgment, more laughter, but all still hinging on my self-image. My favorite line in *Trading Places* is "Looking good, Billy Ray! Feeling good, Louis!"[20] It's so gratifying that in my fifties I'm able to say this to myself in the mirror and actually mean it.

I've already started to change my self-image. It hasn't been without some struggle, but the work is worth the time and energy it takes. Shaming, judgment, and prejudice do not do anyone any good when you let that into your soul. If it festers too long, it will only lead to ugliness and hate. However, when you flip the switch and begin to love yourself, you'll begin to see your potential, embrace your uniqueness, stop living in fear, and grow. You'll receive an immediate mental health boost and build confidence. It's so impactful on our health and wellness and imperative that we develop a more healthy body image.

Where do we start?

It takes work to break this cycle of thinking, and it's best when you concentrate on yourself first.

First thing you can do is to let go of the thought of perfection and there being an ideal standard of beauty or body. We've covered perfection, but looking at your body shape, size, and tone as beautiful is something we can dive into here. Having a healthy self-image is about being kind to yourself, believing in yourself, and showing the world your light. In order to do this you have to be vulnerable. It's a courageous step out from behind the curtain and into view, but one worth taking to grow.

I love what the Dove ad campaign has done for body image. Seeing women of varying shapes, sizes, ages, and colors together in one place as if they were all supporting and respecting of each other is beautiful. We've been fortunate in our lifetime to see the idea of beauty go from heroin chic to this new, more excepting body positivity movement. How amazing was it when we saw real-size models come on the scene in the 90s? That type of representation really helps us all develop a more positive self-image. I love the song "Free Your Mind" by En Vogue. The lyrics are a powerful call to be yourself and stop judging others for what they look or act like.[21]

> *Why, oh, why must it be this way?*
> *Before you can read me*
> *You got to learn how to see me*
> *I said*
> *Free your mind, and the rest will follow*
> *Be color-blind, don't be so shallow*

You have to own your skin, be happy with your body type and skin color. It's easier to do this if you stop comparing yourself to others. It's tough to do because comparison is an innate human trait. But just like with the yin and yang, there are positives and negatives to comparison. Having someone to look up to as a mentor or guide is one thing, but when you're comparing your body type to someone else and shaming yourself, putting yourself down for not looking like other people, that's when it's gone awry. It's time to embrace your uniqueness. Find those qualities about you that no one else has and accentuate them for the positives that they are.

You can affirm what you love about yourself by developing some positive self-talk. A great way to do this is to create affirmations. Using affirmations daily will change the way you see yourself and quickly. This is an easy way to develop new thought patterns about body image and how you talk to yourself. Remember, the goal is to be kind to yourself, love yourself, and show yourself compassion and grace. In chapter 3, I had you tell yourself out loud that you loved yourself, just the way you were. If you feel silly about saying affirmations out loud, you can write them down or you can save them to yourself as part of a meditation practice. Whatever works for you, because using your inner voice or the written word is just as powerful. You can embrace the language we used before or you can create your own affirmations. Whatever works!

Self-acceptance happens quickly when you let go of that negative self-talk. Your stress will reduce, and the anguish you feel around holding yourself to an impossible standard will begin to subside. As a side effect, positive self-talk will help you in creating healthier behaviors. You'll naturally want to take better care of yourself by eating better, moving more, being outside, socializing, and loving yourself. It will ripple out and you will begin to see others with a more positive light, too.

Looking for more tangible things you can do right now, while you change your internal conversation? I've got you covered.

If body size has you spiraling, my advice is to remove all of the size tags in your clothing. You don't need that constant reminder always showing up each time you change your clothes, when you're trying to reprogram how you think about your body. This will help you shift from obsessing about the size of your clothes. The question you should ask yourself when shopping isn't, "Does this make me look fat?" The question should be whether you feel comfortable and confident in those clothes. Wearing things that make you feel good may be contrary to the trends of the day, but when you feel good in what you're wearing, your entire vibe will elevate. You won't need to fit in by wearing trendy clothes, because people will be drawn to your confidence not your look. Bust out of that old way of thinking and wear what makes you look and feel great. This simple shift will change your perceptive of yourself and how people see you immediately. Walk into a room feeling great about what you're wearing and how you look and people will see you the way you see yourself.

Another piece of information that might help you is with regards to clothing. All clothing is designed based on one pattern model. This means that with a particular line of clothing, no matter what the size, the shape of the cut is completely identical. If you find a clothing brand with a fit that you just love, this is probably because their pattern model has a similar body type to you. If you are having a hard time fitting into a line of clothing correctly, that is probably because the pattern doesn't match your shape. The trick with ready to wear clothing is in buying a size that fits and then having the clothing tailored to your size. Having your clothing altered doesn't cost much, but the resulting customized shape and fit of your clothing will have you looking better, giving you more confidence in your clothes.

Another quick hit toward creating a healthier body image is to walk away from the scale. Our generation has put so much emphasis on weight that comparing our numbers has become a favorite Gen-X past time. When you stop weighing yourself, you're removing the stigma tied to a number. It no longer defines you. In lieu of using weight to determine health (which it doesn't) you can use waist measurement to keep you on the right track. Using your measurements and letting the fit be your guide, will help you determine what clothes to buy and keep you from obsessing over weight.

Stop spending so much time looking in the mirror. Looking at your reflection for only 10 minutes a day can cause your anxiety to elevate. Instead, spend your time focusing on how you feel and NOT how you look. When you spend less time in the mirror, your confidence level will rise, while keeping that increased anxiety at bay.

When you do look in the mirror, remember to smile. Smiling is a small simple habit that can make big changes in your life. It releases those mood-boosting endorphins and can help you reduce stress, elevate your immune system, lower blood pressure, make someone else's day, and live longer.

The last thing that will help you build a healthier body image is to surround yourself with positive women who are supportive and boost you up for being you. These ladies need to be a part of your own body positivity movement. Hanging out with positive, confident, kind, supportive women will have you feeling good in your body in no time.

Let's be honest, you may have a setback and say something negative about how you look or how someone else looks. If this happens, don't beat yourself up about it. Shift that conversation into a positive observation. You'll find yourself growing and changing the way you talk the more you intentionally shift your words. Instead of saying, "You look great," say, "You look happy."

It's time you feel comfortable in our bodies and good about the way you look. You can concern yourself with how you look and keep yourself small, or can you rise up out of that head space and enjoy your life for who you are. Share your true self with the world, stop hiding your light, and let go of the worry and fear. When you appreciate and love who you are, you're living in your authentic skin, unafraid, and secure in yourself. Remember, we're all beautiful in our own way.

Start changing how you think about yourself by using these prompts to get on the right path:

• Don't look at yourself in the mirror or any reflective surface for an entire day; instead think about how you feel, not how you look.
• Write down one affirmation to help encourage you to love your body.
• Take a week off from the scale, and instead of weighing yourself daily, tell yourself one good thing about you.
• Un-follow one person on social media with whom you've been comparing yourself, and follow one person who inspires you to be a better person.

Literally

/ˈlidərəlē, ˈlitrəlē/
adverb

5. used for emphasis or to express strong feeling while not being literally true. .
Ex. *"I was literally blown away by the response I got."*

(the power of proper nourishment)

The best thing you can literally do for yourself is to get the proper nourishment. Well-being is not just eating better or exercising—it's about finding harmony, health, and contentment in all areas of your life. When I say nourishment, I mean doing something good for yourself, taking care of yourself. Some people would label that as self-care, and that's great, but it's deeper and bigger than self-care. It's about enriching all areas of your life.

The best way to get through midlife is by feeding yourself the good stuff. I'm not just talking food. Of course, that's what everybody thinks of immediately, when you say nourishment. However, I'm talking about nourishing your spirit, your emotions, your brain, your relationships, your career—absolutely everything, including your body. Everything about your life needs proper nourishment. It's time to fill your cup with what can uplift and enhance your life in support of the lifestyle you want.

There are four main areas you need to concentrate on when it comes to nourishing your life: your space, soul, mind and body. We're going to look at all of these, in this order.

When talking about your space and how it nourishes you, we're looking at not only where you spend your time—environment (e. g., the coffee shop where you hang out most of your mornings)--but also how that space enriches or depletes you. I'm sure if you really thought about it, you could picture in your mind a place or setting where you've experienced an emotional response. It may be within your home, or it could be a public space like a church or the DMV. Maybe it was a positive feeling of invigoration or focus, but it may have been a negative feeling of anxiety or fear. Whatever the feeling, nourishment can be found in places that give you a positive emotional response. Strategically spending time in places that uplift and elevate can enrich your life. I kind of touched on this in the previous when I talked about designing your space for well-being, but here I want you to focus on how environments make you feel. When setting up your personal space to nourish your life, you can concentrate room by room and add intentional features and decor elements to provide you with a specific emotional experience. Plants provide you with good air quality and a connection to nature that helps you feel safe and secure. Color can lift the spirit and create a positive atmosphere. A new mattress can help you get a good quality night's sleep, which will boost your mood and act as a springboard into improving all areas of your life for a phenomenal day and physical experience. Each space is purposely built for enhancing a specific area of your life, so designing to an intended task or to support a particular use of the space, will help you nourish all areas of your well-being.

When my husband and I moved into our new home, we intentionally designed our space for calm and healing. I had just left a career and life where I'd spent nine-plus years suffering from chronic stress and burnout. I needed our lives to be as stress-free as possible, so I knew I needed our home to be comforting, tranquil, spacious, and visually soft. I selected a base color of white (okay, there are actually 4 different whites used throughout our space and on different surfaces). I accented with cool blues and greens, beiges, creams, and naturally dark hardwoods for grounding. I added live plants and feminine touches of soft fabrics, jute, and natural ornamentation, using found and heirloom shells from my grandfather's collection. I layered rugs on top of mats and textures on top of textures. Everything was hand selected to be peaceful and rich with relaxing vibe. The important factor in how our home was designed revolved around my need for healing and growth.

As you begin to create your own healthy environment, think about what nourishment you need in order to have the life you long to live. Because you are the master of your domain, you have the ability to design a life of wellness simply by curating colors, textures, furnishings and accessories that make you feel good and enhance your life.

Your home isn't the only space you can improve to nourish your life. Take a moment to look around your office or in your car. You spend so much time in both of these spaces that they are worth a moment of your time. Don't forget about the other places you spend your time, like church, parks, your favorite coffee shop—each is a space that can nourish or not nourish your life. Spending time in a toxic or negative environment can deplete you and be detrimental to your overall well-being. Whenever you're assessing third-space environments, always remember they can immediately impact you. So make a point to spend time in places that enrich your life by helping you focus on strengthening your health and fostering a greater sense of wellness.

From space to soul, we are shifting to another area of your life that needs nourishment. Finding meaning in life is what our soul needs, in order to be good and nourished. Fortunately, we can nourish our soul in a few quick and easy ways.

It may sound way too simple, but finding pleasure and joy in the little things goes a long way to soothe the soul. I don't know if you've heard of the little notion of finding glimmers throughout your day, but it has changed my life. It came out of the need to stop and be present in the moment, more mindful, but finding a glimmer has become way more. A glimmer is when you notice a small little thing that causes you to experience wonder and joy in the simplest way. If we look for those little glimmers each day, it helps us to not only feel more present, but also be more relaxed and appreciate what is all around us in that very moment we chose to look. It's kinda like your little moment of Zen in the day.

Try this: go out today and find one small little thing that is just astounding. It might be in the laugh of a stranger, the smile on your dog's face, or the sparkle on a dewy piece of grass. It could be something in nature, a person, place, or thing, but no matter what it ends up being, take a moment and appreciate it. You may have to look at things a little differently, so open your eyes because you may find a glimmer in the curve of your phone case. Take a moment and pause to really appreciate how amazing life can be. This little small action will nourish your soul and kick-start the nourishing practice that is gratitude.

Being thankful for all you have and all that you are is the road to greater nourishment for your soul. It's not often that we practice gratitude and for that reason it usually seems awkward. When I started, I took it upon myself to figure out what was so special about gratitude. True to self, I also wanted to know exactly how to practice it the right way. Heads up, there isn't a right way. Duh! However, I did find out that the benefits of practicing gratitude are exponential, but the biggest gift is that it makes you feel good. No, really, it increases the positive energy in your life.

I trained myself to carve out a piece of my day to practice gratitude. Making it part of my daily routine has been great. It's rippled throughout my life and has made each day more rewarding. I started my gratitude practice with the simple act of writing down one thing I was grateful for every morning. I would sit down with my journal and write one thing. Although I may have had more things I could have written down, I chose to concentrate on just the one. The more my appreciation for things in my life grew, the more I wrote in my journal. My practice has since evolved into doing additional things like loving kindness-focused meditations, taking time to get of the house to meditate in nature, forest bathing, and so much more. Practicing gratitude has helped me be more present and appreciate my life and everything and everyone in it.

The practice of gratitude will boost your mood, help you move from anxiety to a feeling of peace and calming, and give you a more positive perspective on the world and your life in general. It really does ripple effect through your life. Even in the most challenging of times, you can stop for a moment and bring a little pleasure and focus into your life. If you're looking at it from an even a bigger picture, this type of gratitude not only keeps you present, but it helps you find greater meaning in the crazy imperfection that is life.

I've noticed my gratitude practice has affected those around me, as well. My gratitude, greater appreciation for life, and more positive mindset has made my relationships stronger. As we know, deeper connections reinforce our innate human need to be fulfilled and have a fulfilled life. In chapter 9, we talked extensively about the importance of friendships. It's no joke. When it comes to nourishing the soul, you can find it in the laughter of a friend as you sit down for a good story and a coffee. It's deeply affecting.

Here are some ideas to get you started on creating your own personal practice.

• Say thank you, until you mean it. Thank God, life, and the universe for everyone and everything sent your way. Say thank you, until you mean it. If you say it long enough, you will believe it.

• Try starting your day by thinking of someone you're grateful for as soon as you wake up. It could be appreciating a friend who sends you funny texts, a teacher who recognizes your child's gifts, or the barista who hands you your coffee and shares friendly conversation. Then at some point, thank that person with a text, note or kind word when you see them.

• Keep a gratitude journal. Set aside some time during your day. Pick a time that works for you. Think back on your day or the day before and write down the things that went right. Maybe your spouse took care of a household repair, or you heard your favorite song on the radio, or you saw a double rainbow. You could even count your blessings, such as having certain abilities or clean water to drink, and write those down. Write down whatever comes to mind - it's your journal.

• Guided meditation is another great way to practice gratitude. My favorite is a Loving Kindness meditation that was part of a UCLA study on cultivating positivity. Participants did this specific meditation for 10 minutes each day and researchers found a decrease in depression and social anxiety along with an increase in feelings of love, joy, cheerfulness, gratitude, fulfillment, and kindness. It actually increased instances of these participants going on to work in public service and nonprofits. You can find this specific meditation on the Instant Timer App, along with a ton of other gratitude meditations. You'll be hooked in no time.

• Create a Gratitude Jar (SNAP JAR). I used to do this at work with my team, but the general idea is, you write down something great about someone else on your team or in your family and stick it in the jar. At a designated time, you all get together and read them out loud. It's an amazing experience to be a part of. Talk about a morale booster.

• Give the gift of gratitude. This can be an actual gift or a letter or handwritten note. You just express your appreciation for that person and tell them. You can even do this face to face. It's an incredible experience.

• Pray. If you're spiritual, you know prayer cultivates gratitude. Also, along the lines of prayer, you could count your blessings. Pick a time each day to be in prayer or reflect on what's going right in your life.

• Practice gratitude as a group. When you're sitting at the table with family, take a moment in the middle of the meal to either have everyone say what they are grateful for or have everyone write it down on a piece of paper and then at the end of the meal spend time reading them out loud over pie.

• Let's not forget about the most important gratitude practice... showing yourself some gratitude. You do so much each day, and we seem to always keep pushing but never appreciating all we accomplish. So show yourself some extra appreciation. We do this through self-care. Here are a few ideas: Book a massage or facial, make a gratitude list about yourself, watch a guilty pleasure on TV and get a blanket to settle in on the couch, or create an at-home spa day with a face mask and steam shower. The name of the game is to pamper yourself with self-care.

Deep connections don't just stave off the loneliness or isolated feelings that we may have as we go through life. They actually help us improve our mental health. We've been studying other cultures through longevity hotspots around the world. Researchers and scientists have found people live the longest and healthiest when they develop and nourish deep connections with other people. Nourishing friendships is good for the soul and your health.

Most importantly, showing yourself a little compassion is really what heals and grows the soul. I can't express this more. We need to show ourselves some grace. We can't expect ourselves to be it all, know it all, do it all, have it all, because life just doesn't work that way. For this very reason, we need to show ourselves some compassion, especially when changing our lives for the better. It doesn't come easily, but it is worth the journey. Compassion can go along way to healing, nourishing, and growing into a better version of ourselves.

To nourish the soul, you need to also nourish your mind. This is where we may dive back into a little stress management conversation from chapter 2. Stress puts a lot of pressure on our overall health, but especially our mental health. It alters our brains, impairing learning and thought capacity, killing brain cells and making us more prone to anxiety, depression, and illness. If we can successfully manage our stress and lower our stress levels, then we can improve our cognitive behavior and heal impairments. We can nourish our mind in a few ways. Through continued learning, whether learning about yourself and learning about things that interest you, you can spark and create new neural pathways in your brain. Enriching your mind by learning new things increases your mental health and strengthens your cognitive function.

When I moved to Louisville, I was moving to a city that I knew nothing about. A city where everything was completely different, including the city layout. Nothing was on a grid, which certainly threw off this typical Virgo's perfect plan. I had to learn new routes, areas of the city, and a new city structure. We didn't have the Google Maps of today. What's a Gen-X girl to do, but get out a trusty map? So, I got myself a map of the city and posted it to the fridge. Every time I left the house, I would look on the map to see where I had to go, and then I would try to find a route to get me there. When I'd leave the house, I'd leave the map behind, get in the car, and use my memory to navigate and find my way to my destination. I got lost a few times, but I learned new secret ways to get places and enriched my brain function exponentially. I did this without being dependent upon technology or someone else to get me around. Now, I know that city like the back of my hand, as if I had been born there. It worked so well that when we moved to a Naples, I picked up a local map and hung it on the fridge. I've learned so much, but now I'm also navigating increases in traffic flows seasonally and what time of the day will be the easiest to get around. I tell you all of this as an example of how to nourish your mind by learning new things.

If you're still not sure of the power of the brain, think about it this way. How many telephone numbers did you know by heart when you were in high school? I mean seriously, we knew everyone's phone number, and we didn't have to write it down. We memorized it. We knew it. I bet if you were asked today, you could still recite your high school phone number and probably your best friend's phone number without a beat. I don't know if it's right for me to share this, but my high school phone number was 769-6965. My brain will never forget it, because it was entrenched in my mind. A new neural pathway was created in my memorizing that phone number. I'm here to tell you it's good for your health to learn new things and if you don't have any idea of where to start take a dance class or get lost in your home town. Whatever way you choose, your brain will stretch and strengthen a little bit. You'll be amazed at what happens.

Last but not least, we're finally talking about nourishing your body. There are four ways to nourish yourself that we haven't already discussed. They are hydration, nutrition, activity, and rest.

Let's start with hydration because this is the one I always harp on. It is so important to hydrate our bodies. We need water to sustain life, help our organs function, nourish our cells, ensure our joints function, regulate the bodies temperature, and eliminate waste. The human body is made up of mostly water, so it's kind of obvious that we need ample water, replenished daily. Hello, 60% of our entire body is water. We are all little floating balls of water, so it makes sense that we need to replenish that water. Obviously, it's the amount we need that has become so confusing. An easy way to understand how much water you're supposed to have each day is to take your body weight and cut it in half. That is the amount of ounces of water your body needs each day. Easy peasy!

I'm not talking about hydrating with your garden-variety tap water. You need unprocessed natural water with natural minerals. You're looking for natural spring water or mineral water to quench your thirst. You might be asking yourself, why is this so important? Well, it's important for proper hydration to have certain minerals with your H2O. These minerals are more commonly known as, electrolytes. You're looking for sodium, calcium, potassium, magnesium, phosphate, chloride, and bicarbonates. Let's be honest, you're not going to want to worry about all that when you're thirsty. The easiest way to ensure you are properly hydrated without all the worry is to drink mineral and spring water. Like everything in this world, not all waters are created equally. It is important that you know the source of your water. You should also know that not all spring or mineral water tastes the same. I know this sounds crazy, but it's true.

Have you ever heard of a water sommelier? Trust me it's a real thing. There are only a few of these professionals in the world today, but that may quickly change given the fact we are all so obsessed with all things health and wellness. Martin Reese is my current favorite, because he has some great videos on Instagram and has a wonderful way of describing why "not all water is water." There are more than 4,000 different brands of spring, mineral, and artisan water. The flavor and sometimes price are based on mineral content levels, source, and even how it's bottled. It is fascinating, so I encourage you to experiment on your own and try different waters. If you don't know where to start, I like Saratoga, Topo Chico, and Gerolsteiner to name a few. Your choice now is still or sparkling and flavor profile. There's not one that's better than the other, but whatever you do, hydrate your body and replenish the water you lose every single day.

You can hydrate the body by drinking good water or by eating water-rich foods. This is one of the best ways to hydrate, while also getting the proper nutrition for your body. High-water content foods include foods like watermelon, cucumbers, oranges, berries, lettuce, carrots, celery, even boiled eggs. The list goes on and on, so all you need to look for are foods that contain a lot of water. Begin by hydrating and then move full steam ahead to nourishing your body with the proper nutrition. We're talking real food like fruits, veggies, healthy whole grains, nuts, seeds, lean proteins, and healthy fats—all necessary for nourishment of the human body.

The human body needs two different types of nutrients: macronutrients and micronutrients. I'm going to hit you with some quick learning. Macronutrients are your carbs, protein, fats, fiber, and water. Micronutrients are your garden-variety vitamins and minerals. It's that simple and easy. Not too crazy complicated to understand, and whether you like it or not, the body works when it has the proper portions of each. I'm not going to have you count your macros and micros although I do know someone who does. I will tell you how important it is to get healthy carbs, fats, proteins, fiber, vitamins, and minerals in your body every day. If you're like me, you don't need one more thing to stress over. I'm not here to give you a diet or a plan or a percentage or any of that junk. I am going to leave you with one thing: if you eat a wide variety of fruits, vegetables, whole grains, nuts, seeds, legumes—which are beans (pretentious, I know)—and lean proteins like fish—specifically cold-water fish for the omega-3's—then you will get all the proper nourishment you need. You'll also gain antioxidants, anti-inflammatories, and nutrition that fights, repairs, and prevents chronic illness. All you need to do is to stick to a wide variety of real food.

On the flip side, we need to eliminate processed foods and beverages from all meals. This could be hard to understand for a generation of latchkey kids who grew up on microwave popcorn, pizza rolls, and other convenience foods. Think of it this way, just don't eat things made in a lab or a warehouse and you should be good. It's been helping me change how I nourish my body. If you want your body to work properly, you have to give your body what it needs to function. If you fill it with junk, it will work like a piece of junk, but if you fuel it with nutrient-rich foods it'll run like a charm.

I have been fortunate to spend years working in the local foods movement with family farmers. Junk food is not just junk for us, but it also takes a toll our environment through damaging farming practices that are depleting our planet's natural resources. I could go on and on, but if we want to get all Gen-X about it, we could buck the system and take this moment to be done with eating this poison and stand up for ourselves by eating real food. You don't have to go all granola and start growing all your food, making bread and ketchup from scratch, because nobody has time for that. What I am saying is, start reading the labels on that you're buying. Know what goes in your food and where it comes from. Maybe you can find yourself a good bakery and baker who knows how to make whole-grain bread without all the junky ingredients. It's important to know what you're putting in your body. If you do nothing else, read your ingredients label and reach for the fresh food. That's all that you need to do. I swear when you start eating the good stuff, you're not gonna be able to stop. The more you feed your body real food, metabolic programming will take over and your body will begin to crave what it needs and your taste will change to match your cravings.

I'm not saying that you can't ever have cake or steak again. You should make those foods a treat, something for a special occasion. Stop making those junk foods your main source of nutrition because they do more harm than good. Shift your thinking, when it comes to what you're putting in your body. The old adage it true, you are what you eat. You've got to fuel yourself and eat things that make you feel good, give you energy, help you sleep, and balance your hormones. If you do that, you're gonna be on your way to being fully nourished.

After you've filled your body up with fuel, you've got to burn it off, and that is where activity comes in handy. Moving your body nourishes your body, because it activates the release of nitric oxide in your system. Nitric oxide is the natural chemical that opens up all the little cells that support all of your organs, your immune system, and every system in the body. It is one of the most amazing ways to nourish your body. The only thing you have to do is move a little bit. And when I say a little bit, you just need moderately raise your heartbeat for 20 minutes a day. Amazing, but that's all your body needs. This doesn't mean you have to go to the gym, because, oh Lord, we don't need to be all crazy workout queens up in here. If you do want to go to the gym, wonderful. The gym is a great place to move your body. However, you can move your body by dancing in your kitchen, doing a morning stretch off the side of your bed, taking a yoga class, going for a walk on the beach or in the park, or sitting on the swings at a park and swinging away. Movement constitutes all forms of motion or ways to get your body's heart rate up and muscles pumping. Your body will thank you for the release of nitric oxide, enhanced cardiovascular health, increase in strength, and improved flexibility you give it. It was made for movement. Otherwise, why would we have all of these amazing joints, tendons, and movable parts? The bonus: when you release nitric oxide on a consistent basis, your body continually releases nitric oxide, whether you're moving or not. The faucet is turned on, and you'll continually nourish your body by the slightest bit of movement. It's amazing! The myth that you have to always be exercising at the gym for hours to really get the benefits of moving your body is totally false. It just takes a little bit of activity. You don't have to do it consistently. You can do a few minutes here and a few minutes there, whatever it takes.

People often ask me what I recommend. What's the best exercise? What program should I be in? Let me tell you, the only thing you need to do is whatever you will do. Get active in doing something you like, something that you will do. No need to depend or focus on what everybody else is doing, just move in a way that you like and have fun with. Seriously, the best exercise is the one that you'll do, bottom line. I love what Jane Fonda says in her workout book: "No distractions. Center yourself. This is your time!" I'm gonna tell you one thing, Jane may be the queen of workouts, but the girl's got it going on when it comes to self-awareness and care too. This is exactly how you should view moving your body. It's your time, no distractions. Do what you need to do, your own way.

After you've taken the time to hydrate your body, feed your body, and move your body, the next thing you need to do is rest your body. Concentrating on rest is somewhat of a lost art. It's lost on most of us because we are constantly in a go-go state of mind. Rest is one of the best ways you can nourish your body. So much so, I've spent the entire next chapter talking about it. One thing I want to point out before we jump right in, it's important to rest your body and give it time to heal, slow down, and regenerate itself every day. This is why we sleep and it is one of the things that most of us are lacking, especially in midlife and perimenopause. We struggle with insomnia and unrest due to our crazy schedules or stressed-out days. It's the one area we need to spend more time on and talk more about. Get ready and pull out your pillows, because in our next chapter, we're talking about the importance of rest.

One thing I feel I need to mention before we move on would be that there are those things that make a toxic impact on our lives, too.

On top of nourishing your body, you have to also remove those things that are depleting you. There are toxic influences like, junk food, stress, toxic relationships, environmental toxins, in activity, self-doubt, shame, fear, loneliness–––the list goes on and on. The important thing to understand is that we need to stop feeding ourselves junk food, lower our stress, remove toxic relationships, remove toxins from our our homes, and stop criticizing ourselves and being overly critical of everything we do. We need to stop keeping ourselves from being healthy at all costs.

With regards to your space, we're talking environmental toxins. Whether you know it or not, in just about everything in your home, there's some sort of chemical. It could be in the glue holding your table together, the stain-resistant fabric on your furniture, or in the paint on your walls. It doesn't stop there. Take a minute and look at the ingredients of your cleaning, skin care, and hair care products—not to mention your makeup and on and on and on—you'll find toxic chemicals in most items you use on or around your body. In most cases, the U.S. allows what they call Generally Regarded As Safe (GRAS) chemicals in products. These chemicals are toxic, but because the level are so low government regulations stipulate that they are safe for human consumption or topical use. Therefore, they're allowed in our products. These chemicals can be neurotoxins or hormone disruptors and can cause chronic illnesses such as breast, ovarian, and skin cancers. So it's important we understand what is in our products and consider how they could deplete our health when we're deciding what we're going to use in or around our homes or on our bodies.

Not too long ago, I started to take a look at my hair care products. That led me down a never-ending rabbit hole. I jumped in head first, because I had been concerned about my increased hair loss in midlife and perimenopause. I knew some of it was stress-related, and I also knew hair loss was a symptom of menopause; but I couldn't really put a finger on what else may be causing it. I was anxious to find out what was causing it, so I looked to my products. When I started to dive deep, I found out my products contained several highly toxic ingredients, and several more that were banned by the European Union. This sent me on a journey into all of my products, from my nail polish to my lotions, body wash, and makeup. Everywhere I turned, I was finding unbelievable chemicals in the ingredients of my products. I already knew about the toxins in household products and those used in the building industry, because I'd studied with the U.S. Green Building Council. However, I was amazed to find highly toxic chemicals in the hair and body products I use on a day-to-day basis. I had been using my shampoo and conditioner for years without a clue as to what was lurking below. I found several neurotoxins and direct hormone disruptors, which I knew were wrecking havoc on the chemical balance of my scalp. It goes without saying that I threw everything away and started fresh with chemical-free products. Since that day, I've noticed slow but steady hair regrowth happening, and I am happy to say my hair has never looked better.

Now, I don't advise that you send yourself down this rabbit hole lightly, but I do think you should think about what you're using on your body. I learned years ago that 4% of everything you put on your body goes into your body. You also need to use caution with airborne products like sprays and foams you use to clean your home, because those chemicals get into the air and reduce the air quality in your home. This is also true of what you bring into your space, from plants that may have mold in the soil to decorative items made with plastics and glue; even your mattress can be an issue. If you haven't noticed, most mattress companies recommend leaving your new mattress to "settle" for a period of at least 48 to 72 hours before you sleep on it. Most mattresses are made with polyurethane foams, synthetic latex, and other man-made, chemical-laden products. Those materials need time, after being released from the plastic covering, to do something called off-gassing. This is the release of chemical fumes. Mattress manufacturers warn consumers to not sleep on a product while it's off-gassing because exposure to the chemical fumes may be hazardous, causing you to get sick. Think about the impact this has on your indoor air quality, and if you're like normal Americans, you don't probably have a filtration system on your HVAC system to clean the air of such intense chemicals. Poor air quality can deplete your health,

Poor water quality can do the same. There are hazardous contaminants, like chemicals and dangerous microorganisms, in even the best municipal water systems. From our drinking water to our showers and even irrigation systems, exposure is possible. Over time, with increased exposure, your health can become depleted. If you remove the potential for harm by filtering your water, you can eliminate another negative impact on your health. I recently added a filtered shower head to my shower to ensure my scalp and skin were not being exposed to additional toxins. I tell you all of this not to freak you out, but to say that we are surrounded by anti-nourishing things, so it is even more important that we nourish ourselves thoroughly, in order to combat the impact of external toxins.

I know it's hard to determine what healthy really means and what proper nourishment really looks like these days. It seems that everyone with a social media account is giving out health and wellness information and telling you what you should and shouldn't be doing to live a healthier life. With all the health and wellness noise out there it comes down to the basics. Treat yourself write, nourish your basic needs, and you'll find you can't go wrong.

Before you move on, take a moment to nourish yourself properly by following these simple prompts:

• Hold your own private water tasting. Grab a few mineral or spring water varieties and give them a taste. Find the one that best suits you and get yourself a case.
• Take a walk this evening and find one piece of nature you think is beautiful. Spend a little time admiring all the fine details and be grateful for the glimmer you've experienced.
• Drive or walk a new route to work or your favorite place without the use of technology,
• Go to the organic or global produce section and try a new fruit this week.

Raise the Roof

/rāz/ /$T̲Hē$,$T̲Hə$/ /rōof,r̆oof/
idiom

1.phrase used to express a desire to get a party started. Often
followed by the phrase "off the hook."
Ex. "Let's raise the roof until this party is off the hook!"

(the value of rest and recuperation)

It's been quite a while since I've raised the roof or anything close to
the type of partying I did in my twenties, thirties or even my forties.
In fact, it was a struggle this year to stay up until midnight for the
New Year's Eve celebration. Thank goodness the televised coverage
included a giddy Anderson Cooper and drunk Andy Cohen. When did
"party til the break of dawn" become "toes up at 10"? I feel like I'm
constantly having to battle this crazy expectation of always having to
be on, going strong, and having it all together. Your mind body and
soul need to rest, recuperate, and regenerate, in order to function
properly. Sleep is the word!

I don't know about you, but I entered midlife head-on, like a
speeding train hitting a wall. I didn't know what was happening to my
body or my brain—sleepless nights were just the beginning. Have you
ever felt this way? Whether you experience sleepless nights or not,
debilitating fatigue and breakdowns from lack of sleep affect 40-50%

of midlife women. Our culture tells us the female midlife experience is irrelevant—live with the hand you're dealt and settle into becoming old ladies. Even if we wanted to, changing our midlife experience feels as difficult as changing how we age. And how could we possibly do that, right? The reality is, we have the power to do both. A good night's sleep is just the beginning. Prioritizing sleep is crucial to your well-being, and optimizing your lifestyle may hold the key to reclaiming the rest you need and deserve.

You either get 7-9 hours of restful sleep or you don't. In my experience, there are a lot of things that can get in the way of a good night's sleep: how you spend each day, what you eat, how you deal with stress, hormonal changes that come with the entire menopausal transition, and the natural aging process, to name a few. Therefore, we not only need to understand how we sleep vs. the natural sleep cycle, but we need to understand how we live too. In my past life, I was a horrible sleeper, and I actually spent a few years suffering from insomnia. Once I was aware of how different I was sleeping, along with how my lifestyle affected my sleep, I was able to shift a few things around, take control, and sleep better. We need to understand our sleep story (how we sleep and live) in order to improve upon our sleep and ultimately our quality of life.

Why do we sleep? Honestly, have you ever really thought about why? The sleep cycle is a magical thing that bears a little explanation. Sleep is a cycle of four repeating stages: three stages of non-rapid eye movement (NREM or quiet sleep) and one rapid eye movement (REM or deep sleep) stage. Each time you cycle through all four of these stages, you fall more deeply into restorative sleep. An entire cycle lasts about 70-90 minutes, but it repeats 4-6 times a night. Spoiler alert: It's normal for your body and mind to wake up momentarily at the end of each full cycle, but most people won't even notice when it happens. In Cycle 1, you transition from awake to sleep before moving into Cycle 2, where your brain processes the memories of the day and organizes information. Cycles 3 and 4 allow the body to heal, repair itself, restore cells, regulate hormones, fight infection and illness, discard waste, and get ready for the new day.

Now that you have a better understanding of how and why we all sleep, it's time to take a look at how *you're* sleeping. I'm sure you're somewhere on the scale between "like a baby" and "what's sleep?" Whatever your current condition, it's good to really dive into what you're experiencing night after night. It's also good to get really clear on what and how you want to be sleeping. I remember lying there and wishing I could zone out enough to drop into a deep sleep so I could relax my body entirely and wake up refreshed. We should be looking at the quality of our sleep to provide that very feeling. It's more quality over quantity, but when we talk about quality, it seems that nobody really knows what that means. You really want sleep or resting time that is healing, restorative, and gives you the feeling of being energized when you wake—feeling completely rested and more alive. Understanding how you want your sleep to make you feel can be a benchmark and goal when helping yourself find your way to a more healing rest.

Surprise! There very well may be things working against you. We know that before, during, and after menopause, quality sleep can be a challenge for both internal and external reasons. It's always good to know what you're working against, so let's take an inventory. Review this list and circle all challenges that you're experiencing right now.

- Hot flashes (a.k.a. night sweats)
- Sleep Apnea due to hormonal changes
- Depression/Anxiety
- Insomnia
- Stress
- Existing medications
- Restless Leg Syndrome
- Racing mind
- Heartburn/Indigestion

As aging women, we'll experience hormonal imbalance and frequent fluctuations, which cause two thirds of the issues on the above list. Don't go down a shame spiral if you circled more than your share of this list. It's super common that we experience several of these sleep challenges in midlife. There are also other factors that may disrupt or prevent good sleep. Those can vary depending upon your particular lifestyle, but don't discount the food you eat, how active you are, any anxiety or depression you're feeling, a bad mattress or cluttered bedroom, physical pain due to an injury—or maybe your kids are a pain. Whatever the case, external factors like light, noise, smells, and sounds could influence how you sleep. It's good to make a list of those, as well.

You might be asking yourself what happens if you don't get good sleep (besides being completely exhausted). Obviously, fatigue can cause all sorts of issues in your life, from not being able to function at work to not paying attention when you're driving your kids to soccer practice and all sorts of issues with your physical health. It's also tied to emotional and mental health. Not getting enough sleep can cause your brain to function improperly, and increase your risk of disorders like dementia. Quite frankly, lack of sleep can cause everything to be worse from the stress you're experiencing to your hormone imbalance. It's imperative that we get the proper amount and quality of sleep, so our mind and body can function properly.

One more thing you might find interesting about sleep is related to weight loss. Restless sleep throws off the hormones that regulate cravings and appetite, but it also inflames your system and results in the body holding on to excess fat. The more quality sleep we get, the more our hormones are balanced, preventing excess fat from sticking around and helping us to keep it off. In order to do this, we need a good sleep routine. If we allow it, sleep can fight inflammation, repair daily wear and tear, keep our brains alert, improve our memories, help us maintain a healthy weight, regulate our hormones, and replenish our cells.

Now, it's time to build a personal sleep routine, so you can sleep better and longer, be more refreshed each morning, rejuvenate and regenerate your body naturally, and redefine how you sleep.

The best place to start is to explore things you can do to improve your sleep. As you probably imagined, there are a ton of ideas out there and, of course, gimmicks, potions, and unfounded advice to sift through. I'll make it easy by sharing a few I adapted from Dr. William Sears. He wrote an entire chapter in his book, *Prime Time Health*,[22] on easy to activate, tried and true tips for getting a good night's sleep. I'm sure you can find a few good nuggets to try out from my list.

1. Move in the morning
2. Consume sleep-enhancing foods (i.e., salmon, pumpkin seeds, tofu, sesame seeds, almonds, beans, and oatmeal)
3. Lose the after-dinner drink (no alcohol)
4. Reduce the caffeine to only mornings
5. Sleep naturally, between 10PM and 6AM
6. Plan for a stressless evening
7. Have a set bedtime
8. Have a set routine
9. Design your bedroom for optimal sleep
10. Take a warm bath or shower
11. Blow your nose to keep oxygen flowing
12. Keep track of snoring/breathing issues
13. Listen to relaxing music or sounds
14. Use lavender oil or spray on pillows
15. Wake up naturally (no alarm clocks)

To achieve optimal sleep each night, you need to create a complementary lifestyle routine. Mine starts with a sleep alarm. I set my phone to alert me each evening of the time I want to begin getting ready for bed. I use this notification as kind of a last notice. My intention is to get to bed sometime between 10 and 10:30PM. When I head upstairs, I make sure everything is shut down, cleaned up, and put away with all of my to-do items either crossed off or tabled until tomorrow. I usually do my typical hygiene routine with brushing my teeth, putting my hair up, and washing my face. However, the last thing I do before I get in bed is use the bathroom. This midlife trick has helped me on more than one occasion. Once I'm in bed, I check my technology and make sure my do-not-disturb is on.

At that moment, I start my meditation routine. Currently, I'm using a binaural beats meditation to help me fade off to sleep. Quite honestly, it takes me only a few seconds into that meditation and I'm fast asleep. It's worth noting that my technology usage in the bedroom is limited and that is on purpose. We rarely ever watch TV in the bedroom. In fact, it wasn't until recently that we even had a TV in our bedroom. Actually, my husband puts his clothes for the next day in front of the TV, so it never gets turned on.

As for setting an alarm, I don't. After I left my corporate job, I decided that I didn't want to be alarmed out of sleep anymore, so I got rid of all alarms in the bedroom. It's really interesting because both my husband and I now wake up naturally on our own cycles. He wakes up about an hour and a half earlier than I do—and let's face it, partially because the dog is licking his face to go out. I get up at the same time every day and sometimes earlier with the sun. It works beautifully. I get up feeling refreshed on a natural high and ready to face my morning. It's not alarming. It's not shocking. I don't have to hit snooze, and on the rare occasion that I have to get up earlier than my natural cycle, I can feel the stress and anxiety that an alarm causes me when I wake from sleep.

You have to find your own routine, the one that works for your lifestyle and your needs. My routine may not fit your life, but it can inspire you to find one that does.

Start by looking at my brain dump of ideas listed here. This will get you one step closer to designing a unique sleep routine to soothe your soul and re-establish your ideal sleep cycle. Try some new things out and develop a way of calming and setting yourself and your space for restfulness.

- Use the bathroom right before bed
- Avoid electronics after getting in bed
- Read a book in bed
- Lower room temperature to 65 degrees Fahrenheit
- Stick to a regular time to bed and wake
- Stretch for a nightly "cool down"
- Take a nature walk –or move outside daily
- Have a warm/cool shower before bed
- Turn on a fan or have one at the ready
- Relax with a warm drink
- Use a guided sleep meditation or say a prayer
- Do a relaxing yoga nidra practice
- Limit nicotine, caffeine and alcohol
- Turn up the sleep sounds
- Optimize your bedding—lightweight blankets, satin

pillowcase, wicking sheets
- Eat sleep-enhancing foods daily
- Think happy thoughts—don't go to bed angry
- Take an evening after-dinner walk
- Write down all the things you are grateful for
- Spray your pillow or bedding with lavender

This brings us to assessing your sleep environment, your sacred space, your sanctuary, your inner sanctum, your boudoir, your bedroom. As a wellness design expert, I know your interior environment is a key factor in your health and well-being, not to mention your sleep quality. In my experience, there are interior elements in a space that can either strengthen or disrupt the natural biological rhythms of the entire sleep experience. Because we know how certain things influence us, we can design a space that allows our circadian rhythm to align with our health goals.

There are several factors that directly affect your sleep. Think about it like you would any other space, by using your five senses. You want your sleep space to be a place of wellness, calm, and peace, so it needs to be set up to support a goal of rest, recuperation, and rejuvenation. So how do we do that?

The best place to start is with lighting. Our cycle of energy is intertwined with the sun. A room filled with natural light not only illuminates your space, but also triggers the wake/sleep cycle and positively affects your emotional well-being. However, sleep can be disrupted by even the slightest bit of light (I see you, phone charger). Whether you need to block the light entirely or not, curtains are a good way to help you keep your circadian rhythm in check. We also have to consider lighting within the room. We light our space according to the task at hand. This means overhead lighting should be dimmable, and bedside lamps should be used for reading. If you need, you can always use a ceiling fan for extra comfort in helping to adjust the temperature. This works especially well if you have become a victim of night sweats. Remember to always lower the temperature or at least adjust it to what you find comfortable for a better night's sleep.

Ideally a bedroom should face east or south, so you can wake naturally with the rising sun. When this isn't possible, you can ease anxiety with proper furniture placement. Make sure to face your bed, so when lying down you are looking toward the door. This will allow you to feel safe and sound all night. Soft blankets, smooth sheets, satin pillowcases, and a supportive mattress and pillows all play a role in providing the perfect scenario for sleep. Comfort is the name of the game when it comes to proper bedding. Try linen sheets. They're long-lasting and are cool against the skin. The bedroom should be a place to heal and relax. Create a space within the room where you can retreat with a good book or simply to breathe, building upon the idea and experience of sanctuary. Natural materials such as wood and plants have been shown to invoke a feeling of peace and calm within a room. Live plants provide a vibrant life source with the added benefit of being natural air purifiers. Don't forget about sound machines, aromatherapy, a good book, or meditation practice to help you set the stage for a soothing night sleep. Be mindful of what you need to help you relax and drift asleep.

I mentioned it earlier when sharing my sleep routine, and it may seem impossible, but research has found that removing the TV and other technology from your bedroom will improve your sleep. If possible, find a place away from your bed to store and charge your tech. Good luck to all you nighttime scrollers out there. While you're removing the TV, take away some of the extra clutter that often accumulates on the tops of the dressers and nightstands. Clutter can cause a subconscious reaction that leads to increased anxiety, so the less clutter the better.

One last thing to consider that is often overlooked—color. This is a key element to the experience of a space. Some colors are cool, others are warm—some enliven, while others calm. While color is a key element, it is always a deeply personal experience. When designing your sleep sanctuary, you want to choose a color or combination of colors you find the most relaxing. To calm and heal, you'll want to explore cool blues and greens. Both colors are very comforting and calming, but if you struggle with them, look to creams, whites, and light camel beige colors for grounding and relaxation.

Don't look at me all crazy. I don't expect you to go out and do all of this today for a great night's sleep tonight. I implore you to sit a moment, assess your sleep behavior, decide how you want it going forward, try a few new things, and eventually create a sanctuary where you feel you can relax and rest awhile.

Here are a couple of prompts to get you ready for a good night's sleep:

• Write down your current nightly routine and see if there is anything missing.
• Try one new thing this week from my brain dump list of ideas.
• Add a little nature to your sleep space with a live lavender plant.
• Clear out the extra clutter in your sleep space or at least organize it so your brain can relax easier each night.

You Rock

/yōo,yə/ /räk/
interjection

1. phrase of praise or encouragement conveying admiration, gratitude, or affection. Often appears in conversations when one has impressed the other; whether it be by a show of one's talent or skill, or generosity and kindness at heart.
Ex. "You're on a good path. You rock!"

(living on purpose)

People are so stuck on the word *purpose* these days. Purpose has become so trendy, attached to corporate trainings, initiatives, and workshops, not to mention longevity factors and reasons for happiness and success. People are just clinging to it to define themselves, not really understanding what having purpose actually means. The real idea behind knowing your purpose is to find meaning in your life and understand your reason for living. It's not about wearing it as a badge of honor so people know who you are. It's way bigger than all that.

It wasn't too long ago that I woke up and said to myself, "I don't think I'm living my true passion." As I began to explore this thought, I realized I didn't really know my authentic self, let alone my purpose in life. I had reached a point in my life where I'd just been following in the steps laid out before me and doing the things I thought I had to do. As with any completely typical Gen-X experience, I suddenly realized my life wasn't fulfilling. In fact, it was the exact opposite of fulfillment. It was sucking my soul dry, and I knew I had to make a change. I identified with this word *purpose* and began a deep dive into what it was. I needed to understand what I felt I needed my life to be and how I wanted to spend it. I thought purpose was a thing that you did and somehow it would define what I was supposed to be doing as a career, but the more I got into the actual meaning behind the word, the more I understood that it was far bigger than a job. Purpose wasn't something that defined me, but something that actually was a part of me. I soon found that having a purpose and meaning in life is a complete godsend. When you are fulfilled living a life that is meaningful, your life and you totally rock!

Let's start at the beginning. Purpose is the reason you do something. In other words, the intention behind your action. It is the thing that gives meaning to everything you do. It's what makes you want to get up in the morning. It's spiritual more than tangible, and for that it is an important part of our overall well-being. Having a life of meaning, being fulfilled, and living your purpose is not only healthy, but has been proven to increase longevity through improved joy, happiness, satisfaction, and hope. Having a higher sense of purpose has been shown to reduce stress and inflammation, as well as lower health risks like heart disease, heart attacks, and strokes. It essentially allows you to live better, healthier, and even longer. Researchers have identified purpose as a vital part of increased longevity. They've found that you're more apt to take care of yourself because, quite frankly, you've got bigger fish to fry and you need to be healthy to see it through.

It's not only just a buzzword in Western culture. Purpose has been identified and explained differently based on cultural ideas and historical timing. The Japanese have a concept called *Ikigai*. The idea is that you have this motivating force or *Ikigai* at your core, from which you gain a reason for living. There are four areas that link to your *Ikigai*. Essentially it's the connection between what you value most and enjoy doing; your strengths and skills; how you can provide value to others; and how you can use all of this to be financially sustainable. When you explore these four areas with curiosity and use your intuition as your guide, you can determine your purpose and how it will manifest throughout all areas of your life.

I think a lot of people get overwhelmed when you start talking purpose because they feel inadequate, like they need to manifest it as some amazing discovery or big thing. In all actuality, though, it could come through as a simple kindness shown to someone. Purpose doesn't have to be a big moonshot. It's really more about knowing yourself and living your truth. No matter what purpose looks like to you, it should lead you to finding fulfillment and a reason for living.

So how can we find our purpose in life?

All you have to do is look around. You'll notice every kind of self-help book known to man, workshops, retreats, conferences, social media posts, and videos ready to help you learn how to find your purpose. Where there is an interest, there's a person out there who can tell you how to do it.

When I was diving into my journey, I picked up a book called *Finding Your Own North Star* by Martha Beck. She walks the reader step-by-step through a self-exploration of who you really are and how to get the life you want. I found out so much about my authentic self by diving deep down and mining all the experiences, beliefs, biases, well-intentioned guidance, and trauma to gain clarity and direction for my life. I explored my identity and passions—things I hadn't thought of in years. It really helped me to get focused on what I wanted for my life. The book was what I needed in that moment as a divining rod for my soul search. However, to be honest, it didn't work for me when I was at another stage of my life story. It had been living on my bookshelf collecting dust for 20 years. I'd started it at an earlier and completely separate time of transformation, but I never finished it. It even had all the little scribbles in it from the last time I had found myself at such a crossroads. They were hilarious to read, a total blast from the past. It took 20 years before I was actually ready and in a place to pick it up again and finish what I had started in my thirties. I tell you all of this to say that what worked for me may not work for you. Moments and situations like having a milestone birthday or nervous breakdown can be a catalyst for you to examine your life and find your purpose. Just like with any personal work, you really need to find the technique or tool that resonates and is instinctual to you.

You'll know when you know. Be open and ready to get to your core "why" and dive deep within your authentic self.

Here's the deal, finding your purpose isn't something that happens quickly. A lot of exploration and some pretty deep dives need to happen for real clarity to be gained. After all, like Miracle Max said in *The Princess Bride*, "You rush a miracle man, you get rotten miracles."[23] We'll do this together, but you'll want to come back and go deeper and deeper, maybe even finding an additional way to explore your purpose. Any way you slice it, we're not in a rush. However, we're here and I've got you captured. I'm sure at this point you're pretty enraptured with my prose. So how about if you get a jump start and we work on a simple purpose exercise together?

You've already worked on understanding your core values (what's important in your life) in a previous chapter, and you've been thinking about a vision for the life you want to lead. Now it's time to look at where you've excelled, previous experiences that have excited you, and what you're naturally good at. Once you explore strengths and passions, then you can look at why this matters most. Obviously, the more you know about yourself, down to the small details, the better. This deeper understanding will help you know your authentic self, in order to pinpoint how your unique gifts can shine out with purpose. This is where your gut instincts will come in handy. Listen for reactions of joy, happiness, and excitement to things you're really passionate about and those things that fill your heart.

Let's not get ahead of ourselves. You first need to identify your strengths, skills, talents, and characteristics that make you able to do those crazy things you can do. Let's face it, it's really hard for us to look at ourselves and say, "Wow, I really do this well" or, "This is my superpower talent." Although difficult, it's worth being a little uncomfortable as you shine the light on yourself to unearth those magical things that make you, you. For this exercise you need to take a little step back, in order to take a step forward.

Flash back to your early childhood.

That little girl absolutely loved _____.

Fill in this blank with everything she was passionate about and loved doing. It's okay if your list is long, she was a fun kid.

Now, flash forward a bit to young adulthood, those teenage years.

Think about those things you were good at and the characteristics you were proud of.

That awkward teenager's best qualities were _____.

Fill in the blank with everything you can remember. These are the tough memories to sift through, so take time to make your list. If it's easier, look at those college years too. You may be screaming, "Oh lord help me," but you're doing this because a quick little assessment of yourself as a kid helps to open up your mind and it enables you to look at yourself in the mirror right now. However, before we get to that, there's another way we can unlock your brain.

Think of your favorite person, your support person, your rock, that someone you know really well. Start to make a list of their strengths. I'm sure you could come up with a bazillion things that make them amazing. Once you're done coming up with all the amazing things about your friend, flip that question around and look at yourself. What would your friend say about you? What are your "in real life" strengths, right now in this moment? Explore all of the things that make you feel really good when you do them. Take a minute right now and jot down all of the characteristics, traits, qualities, skills, and talents that you have. If you think you don't have a very long list, that's okay. We only asked for a minimum of three values, so just shoot for three strengths. You just need to identify a couple to compliment and combine with your values. After all, you need to know what matters most to you and what skills you have to help you make what matters come true. Number the strengths you have in order of importance to you. Those top three are the traits that make you magical.

There is a connection between our values and our strengths. Your values are what matters to you and your strengths are your skills that help you actualize what matters. When you have a clear understanding of both of these, then look out because you can set any goal, vision, or purpose for living and make it a reality. If you're like me, you may need a way to reference these throughout your day. Don't be afraid to post your values and strengths on your wall or as a screensaver on your computer or whatever way works for you to have them front and center. Every time you think you can't do something, just look at those two things and you'll find the inspiration and motivation you were looking for.

The next thing we need to explore in finding our purpose is the question of our bliss. Time to ask yourself a few more questions. Is there something that you could do for the rest of your life if money wasn't a worry? Is there something that fires you up, excites you, fuels your passion? What really inspires you to be a better you? This is a great time to assess passion, so take everything that is coming to mind and start a list for easy reference.

Because we've had a lot of experiences by now, along with a tremendous amount of ideas, thoughts, and dreams of what we might want to do or what could be cool to try, your list could get crazy long. This is the time where you get to brainstorm and brain dump all that stuff out, so get yourself a few pieces of paper and write down everything you're passionate about. Everything that excites you or inspires you is a potential passion. Let it all spill out and let's get real. Take time to explore what it was about those things on your list that made you feel good. Go deeper. Notice if there are any common patterns or similarities between thoughts. Determine what it is that really motivates you, really gives you a sense of fulfillment. What are the circumstances that make you feel your life is valuable? Take notes on the things that come to mind and how you react to them.

I know you're probably asking yourself, "Why are we talking about passions? I thought we were talking about purpose." Well, these two concepts are seriously intertwined. Knowing your passion is a good gateway into defining your purpose. Passions are those surface interests that get you excited and create those butterflies in your stomach, and purposes are the ones that give you a visceral experience at your core, awakening your authentic self. Heads up, your purpose should feel like your reason for existing. I know that sounds like George McFly in *Back to the Future*: "You are my density, I mean my destiny."[24] It's true. Purpose is a little like destiny, and there's no getting around it.

When you have that list of passions, go through line by line and ask yourself, is this my reason for existence? If the answer is no, it's a passion. If the answer is Hella Yeah, it's a purpose. Remember, passions may be exciting and get those butterflies going, but the deep yearning and drive in your core is your purpose. As you begin to identify passions and purpose, know this is not a numbers game. You're looking for a "rock your core" instinctual feeling.

This exercise should get you well on your way to defining a purpose or something you can focus on that gives your life meaning. If it helps, I once heard purpose described as what you do for other people that makes you unique. That phrase struck me, changing the way I view purpose. When you look at it this way, purpose becomes less of a thing and more of a selfless act or way of being. The transcendence that having purpose provides is what makes life fulfilling. It's beyond what you need and really is more about having a connection to something larger. You may call it the universe, the collective energy, or God. Whatever you choose to name it, know that it is rooted in your belief system. This all makes sense... Purpose lives within the same dimension of wellness as faith and spirituality, known as Spiritual Wellness. With your purpose being steeped in your belief system, your beliefs are just as important to finding and knowing your purpose as everything else we've talked about.

Why is having a purpose so important?

When you combine your values, beliefs, strengths, and passions, you find yourself with a higher purpose or a drive to find the meaning of life. Your purpose is nestled into the same category of wellness where you will find faith or spirituality. Through spiritual wellness you can understand your beliefs and higher purpose, along with your meaning of life, so you know where you fit into this big old existence. It's our nature to want to have meaning put to something and to understand the larger world itself. Obviously, there have been people like Aristotle, Socrates, Nietzsche, Confucius, and Chomsky who have searched for that something more out there in the universe and whose teachings can contribute to understanding your sense of purpose. While it is good to have philosophical perspective to glean from, it is more important that we look for hope and understanding within ourselves. That hope is also a huge part of spiritual wellness and purpose that allows us to grow and develop.

Having a quest for meaning provides a big boost to your mental health. It provides you with the space to flourish, which helps you overcome adversity. Having a sense of a higher purpose or higher power will guide and fuel you through adverse situations, helping you tackle those situations with grace, stay optimistic, and have resiliency. When you dive deep and find that purpose from within, you actually can self-motivate and do things on your own behalf, making you ready, willing, and able to take on anything.

How do I live my purpose?

If you're still struggling with finding or living your purpose, there are a few things you can do to spark the exploration process. Seek out new experiences, things that can stretch you, things that make you take a stance on what you believe and what you don't. You want to try to stretch yourself beyond who you are right now. Try something that makes you excited or can give you a glimpse of a life you're dreaming of. You've already reflected on your own experiences, values, and strengths; hold those dear and use them to better understand yourself. Do some self reflection about who you are. Are you living true to your values and within your strengths? This will help you seek out new and differing perspectives.

Purpose can either inform or enhance your vision for your life while you become your best self. Refer to the vision you are working with or the one you're creating to see if it aligns with the purpose you discovered. Check out where you are now and what you need to do to become fully aligned with your reason for living. Be positive, optimistic, and grateful as you gain clarity around your purpose and how it is your life. It's always helpful to look at life with wonder as you would if you were a kid. In those little moments, you will better understand your purpose and last, but not least, find faith in what will be.

It may help you to take a moment and help others to reset your perspective on what living in purpose looks like. When you do something nice for others, for instance, serve at a food pantry, that feeling you get, the rush of love and kindness that humbles you, the one that rocks you to your core and makes you want to do more for your fellow man, that is a helper's high. It is a spiritually energetic experience tied to your beliefs. For me, it happens when I'm in service of a higher power, a greater good, something bigger than me. I choose to call it God. My belief in God is what gives me hope, what grounds me, assuring me there is good in the world. Having a faith in something is what keeps me from living a life of fear and anxiety in the unknowing and uncertainty. This is a belief that works for me and I know you'll find the beliefs that work for you too. You can easily access what you believe, feel, and hold to be true, this cognitive component that makes you who you are by giving back and being of service to others. It is a great way to explore your purpose and can positively imprint on our behavior and lifestyle.

Values, strengths, and even passions and purpose can change over time. It may be that you become better at something, maybe you enjoy something a little bit more, maybe you're in a different phase or you're interested in something new. It's always good to reassess values, strengths, and purpose, so that you can continue to make sure that you're on the track for the life you want to be living, one of fulfillment and full of meaning.

You can use the same existential questions that we as humans always ask. Who am I? Why am I here? How can I contribute? It's this last question that leads us to identifying purpose. Janice Trachtman said it beautifully in her book, *Catching What Life Throws at You: Inspiring True Stories of Healing*. She said, "Everything is within your power, and your power is within you." Those are words to live by![25]

Get a better handle on living with purpose by using these few prompts to get started:

• Volunteer for your favorite charity. Spend one afternoon in service of others and take note of how that makes you feel.
• Write down a list of things you believe. Once you have your list, ask yourself why you believe that statement it true. Explore the origin and validity of that belief to see if it is something that you really believe or something you've been told to believe. Adjust accordingly.
• Do one new thing this week. Make it something you've been wanting to try for awhile.
• Follow 2 new people who inspire you on social media. Don't forget to also delete 2 people who don't inspire you.

Not

/nät/
interjection

1. following and <u>emphatically</u> <u>negating</u> a statement.
Ex. "Sounds like you know what you're doing... Not!"

(imagining the possibilities)

If you're like me, you may have thought that by midlife you'd have your shit together, be highly successful, have your mansion, with your red corvette, be married to (insert hunky 80s dreamboat here - Jake Ryan), have two adorable kids, and live by the ocean in Italy... NOT!

Who doesn't love a good fortune-telling game? Although a fun way to spend a sleep over, it wasn't real great about setting us up for the reality of a Gen-X life. It might have helped if we'd had more than one career day in high school or if the school counselor did more than her nails every day. Do you remember doing those assessments that told you what you should do as a career, only to be told that an FBI agent isn't really the job for a girl? We were given no direction. Just a good push out of the nest and a hearty "good luck" to get us started in finding our way to an all-too-mundane existence.

If you were one of the lucky ones who knew what they wanted to do after college, then maybe you're living the life you envisioned. If you're like the rest of us, then maybe it's all been one fleeting dream after the other. It might be menopausal brain fog talking, but I think it's time we all gained a little clarity and direction.

Who would you be and what would your life look like if you were living your best life?

I'm sure you probably haven't thought about this in a long time. I mean, it's next to impossible to fit that in with everything else you're trying to juggle. While we're here, let's take a moment to give it a thought.

I was in your position just a few short years ago. I was unrecognizable to myself. I had no idea who I was, let alone whose life I was living. My career path and resume looked like a "Chutes and Ladders" board. I had bounced around, changing direction several times, every time looking for something that was fulfilling, a glimpse of the real me, a way to take one more step closer to an energetic pull I kept feeling in my heart. It sounds dramatic, I know; but it felt dramatic to me, especially in that moment of complete breakdown and burnout. If I wanted to get out of the hole I had created, I knew I had to get clarity around who I was and what I wanted my life to be like.

I did two exercises that really help me focus on what I wanted. First, I took a moment to write down my worst-case scenario day. Believe it or not, this was the easiest thing to do. After all, I was living my worst day every day. My story spilled out of me like water out of a fire hose. Once I was finished unloading all of my angst, I took a moment and read the entire thing over again. As I did, I focused in on the emotional responses and gut feelings I experienced while reliving my worst day. It was a toxic soup of post traumatic stress, only it was my current daily scenario.

Okay, take a deep breath and shake that negativity off. Here's where we take a turn for the better. The second exercise I explored was to slow down, dream, and write down my best-case scenario day. I pulled out all the stops. It wasn't much of a chore to think of a day better than what I was living. After all, I was at my personal rock bottom. I wrote, wrote, and wrote all about my best day, from the moment I would wake until when I laid my head down on my pillow at night. I added in all sorts of detail with locations, people, activities—even what I ate for breakfast. It was all there in black and white. The very best day I could ever imagine. When I read what I had written, I was overcome with feelings of joy, peace, wonder, elation, and bliss. I couldn't believe the vast difference in the two different day scenarios. Then I thought, "Why am I living my worst day over and over again?"

By writing these two days out, I was given a gift. I was allowed to imagine just for a moment what the life I dreamed of could actually look like in motion. This is a powerful place to be, since if you know what you want, you can focus in on it in order to figure out what you have to do to get you there.

So what is your story?

If you're up for it, take a moment to write out your worst and best day, compare the two, and imagine what it would be like to actually live your best life. Once you have this vision in mind or in writing, then you can gain more clarity on how to make this dream a reality.

You can form a personal vision by writing a story like I did or you can create a vision board, Pinterest page, mood board, vision statement, a list, or whatever works for you to keep you motivated and on track. It should give you hope and be aspirational, inspirational, and completely personal and in line with your authentic self. Whatever the form you choose to use to get clarity on what you want, do something that resonates with you and allows you to express yourself wholly.

What do you do now that you have a clear vision?

Ask yourself... If I were 100% certain I was going to be living the life I envisioned by the end of the year, what would I be doing today? Knowing where you're going is just as important as knowing how you're going to get there. A good plan, outline, strategy, or map can help you reach your weight loss goals, lower your stress, give you more time to spend with family or take care of yourself. Whatever your vision is of you at your best most successful self, a good wellness plan will help you step-by-step to move forward with clarity and focus.

The question I asked myself to get started was a simple one. What would I have to actualize to live my vision every day?

Fortunately, my husband was the love of my life and a part of my best life vision. Nothing to change there, but I did want to make the time I spent with him better. I also needed to figure out my purpose. In order to do that I began to peel back the onion to find who I really was at my core, my authentic self. I got to know my values and my strengths. Not to mention, I alleviated stress, which led to taking better care of myself and a whole slew of other things that, as I got closer, needed to be addressed so that I could actually live that vision I had for myself.

I picked away at it slowly, working on the things I was ready to undertake and setting small goals to help me get closer and closer to a better reality. I had to change habits, develop new routines, and build boundaries and safety nets, while assessing everything in my life to learn how I could have it better. I tried a ton of things on for size, being mindful of my emotions and gut instincts, noticing when things felt right or wrong for me. I learned so much about myself and couldn't believe it took me until midlife to realize that my life was my choice. I had a discussion with a friend who asked me why I didn't have to do something she thought I should do, and my response to her was a simple, "because I'm an adult."

I am clear. My life is of my own making, and if I want to have it different, it's my choice. Because everything in my life is my choice, I am the architect of how it plays out. I always have the choice to say no if something doesn't align with my values, beliefs, strengths, purpose, or vision. It's that easy. Through my own efforts, I have been very successful in creating the life I want, and I'm now living it.

Take time to dissect your vision and pull out what has to happen for it to become a reality. Once you have those macro-goals identified, break them down to smaller pieces. Go one further by creating even smaller steps, more manageable micro-goals that you can immediately achieve when you're ready. The key to having the life you want can be summed up with a simple strategy. Focus on what you want to change, ask yourself if you're ready, know what steps you need to get you there, and find a way to ensure you stay true to yourself and on your own path.

Why is all of this so important?

Having clarity about your life enables you to focus, stay calm, stress less, and maintain a sense of certainty about your life. Having a definitive vision is like having a treasure map with a huge X marking the spot. The macro- and micro-goals act as the steps along the way, leading you to the life you're yearning to live. The overwhelming indecisiveness, anxiety, uncertainty, worry, and fear you usually have with change can all be alleviated with every step in place. On average, an adult makes 35,000 decisions every day, so having a map to guide you gives you the confidence and clarity to move forward with focus and prioritized steps to help you get more done without having to make any additional decisions. Success looks like eliminating or cutting back on the decisions we make each day. However, it also looks like having the ability to clearly ideate along the path, evolving instead of standing still. You'll be able to put your time and energy into supporting your values and using your skills as you achieve your goals. You can easily stick with your routines, building upon them with each new step and maybe adjusting or adding ways to keep you healthy and happy. The best reason to have a clear vision is to make your life pleasurable, nourishing, and more manageable.

Start finding clarity in your life by following these simple prompts:

• Think of one word that describes your ideal life and let yourself ruminate on how that feels.
• Go outside and sit in nature to collect your thoughts and clear your mind.
• Stop using social media to hide from reality by taking a technology break. Instead of scrolling, write a list of fun things you want to do over the next year.
• Do yourself a favor and plan out your day the night before by picking out your outfit, planning your meals, and confirming your schedule to take the weight off having to make those decisions first thing in the morning.

Whatever

/(h)wəd'evər/
exclamation

1. said as a response indicating a reluctance to discuss something, implying indifference, skepticism, or exasperation.
Ex. *"Whatever! I'm going to live my life, my way."*

(knowing your authentic self)

Exhausting! Aren't you tired of trying to fit in and be accepted, bending yourself to be something you're not? It's like we were brought up in an era where we were told to be unique and be ourselves, but we were inundated with messages to be like everybody else—from how we dressed to how we spoke—and if you were yourself, you were ostracized for being weird. Our Gen-X youth was a juxtaposition between being part of the *it* crowd, that herd mentality, and being the standout courageous freak. I don't think I ever heard the term authentic used in conjunction with someone's way of being until my forties—let alone understood the courage, joy, and relief that accompany authenticity. Whatever! It's here to stay, and I'm ready to be the most authentic me I can be.

Psychology Today defines authenticity as "Acting according to one's true self and behaving congruently with values, beliefs, motives, and personality disposition."[26] Whether you're just beginning to find yourself or have been working on peeling back the layers for a while, know that you're not the peel—you are the juicy center.

How can you get to know your authentic self?

I watched an interview with Brene Brown recently and she just nailed the answer to this question. She said, "Authenticity is the daily practice of letting go of who we think we're supposed to be and embracing who we are."[27] I took this to mean that you have to look past the person "they" all want you to be and who you thought you were, so you can see who you really are. Somewhere along the way, we've forgotten who we truly are. Mostly, because what we learned was to conform, be a part of the crowd, and hide our true selves, so we wouldn't be judged or ridiculed. We've created this self-concept, how we perceive ourselves, based on our experiences, external influences, and societal demands. We make up stories about who we must be for others, what we see in the mirror, how we show up in the world, what we're capable of, and so much more. We begin to form masks for every occasion, trading them out to fit the moment or the social interaction, all to be the ideal person for what others need. It's tough to come out from behind all those masks, when we fear being met with indifference and skepticism. It's natural that we are reluctant to show our authentic nature and stand up for it in the face of adversity.

When I was in middle school, it might have been fifth grade, I somehow became the target of one of the "popular" girls in my class. I really can't recall the details (brain fog, of course), but I made a comment or statement of some sort about something I believed and it rubbed her wrong. I remember the fear I had as her demeanor changed the moment what I said set in and didn't align with her thoughts. I felt immediate rejection, worry, and shame. As I look back on it now, it was an obvious power struggle for attention and reverence with the group we were sitting with. She smiled coyly and made some offhanded comment, but I knew that was a turning point. Moments later, before the next period, I remember her walking up to me and telling me she was going to beat me up at recess that afternoon. It sounds extreme, but it was Gen-X and that's just what we did. All the sudden, my afternoon was shaping up to be a hair-pulling fist fight. I was petrified. One, because I had no idea why what I said that set her off. I mean, we had been friends five seconds before. And two, I had never fought anyone besides my sisters and definitely not with fists. I didn't have a clue how to fist fight. Immediately, other girls rallied around me for support, but most turned their heads. I even remember her boyfriend coming over to tell me she was going to kick my ass, but that he was sorry. Whatever! Anyway, I dug deep and decided I wouldn't run. I would stand up for myself and be on that playground early and exactly where she wanted me to meet. It took absolutely everything I had within me to be brave and vulnerable, but I went and I waited. In the ball of emotions that was the entire recess, I wrestled with the feelings of bravery and fear, weakness and strength, fight and flight. When the bell finally rang, I was standing with just a couple of friends nearby, by myself. She never showed; in fact, nobody saw her anywhere near the spot she picked or me the entire recess. I was shocked, relieved, and quite frankly, empowered. I stood up for myself and didn't back down to the peer pressure to be a certain way or think like the crowd. It was incredible, but short-lived. Middle school days, like any other moment in time during those formative years, was emotional whiplash. One day you're cool; the next you're not—no reason, just keeping you guessing. I could have used that moment as a turning point to be myself and not back down. However, the pressure was too much, and I didn't have any guidance on how to really embrace my truth like I do today. Oh, the pressure!

Yes, I struggled with being in and out of the crowd after that incident. I wanted the Jordache jeans, Giorgio perfume, Liz Claiborne purse, my hair to be perfectly permed and big, to be cool and sit on the benches in the main hall of my high school. However, I ended up being "normal" with my Sasoon jeans, Love's Baby Soft Spray, no-name bags, badly styled hair, and a wide array of friends and interest. I'm sure that fight (or lack of fight) was what kept me one foot in the cool crowd, but I never was a part of any certain clique. I had a foot in all of them, mainly because of the authentic friendships I had, not because I was always my authentic self. The coolest thing about me was that I was the art chick of my class. Honestly, I never really fully embraced that part of me either. I didn't want to be different. I was too scared to show my true self to anyone and I lived in mediocrity for years, balancing all sides of the coin to "fit in."

It's like that scene in *Pretty in Pink*, where Andie says, "You know, it's so insane that someone you've never met, never talked to can be your enemy. I just want them to know that they didn't break me. If somebody doesn't believe in me, I can't believe in them."[28] Andie Walsh was the picture of strength under peer pressure, but I never had the courage to stay true to myself and stand out and up for myself.

I look back on it today and feel like that girl missed out on so much of her greatness. It's a bummer, but what an amazing learning experience to have had. All that I've gone through, lived, and learned has made me even more incredible today. I'm still gaining insight from all of those tales of woe and the internal struggle to be seen, to matter, to really know myself, so my journey in self-exploration isn't nearly over. Thank God for a crazy college party, a very frank discussion, and a night I will never forget. One evening, during a discussion that may or may not have been fueled by hallucinogenics, this friend looked at me and asked if I was always going to be the doormat or if I could stand up for who I was. I had never had someone be that frank with me before, let alone me being in such an open state of mind to receive such a true analysis. But there it was and I listened. That one moment, one statement, was the catalyst that pushed me out of the box I was living in and toward a journey to find myself before I even knew what the word authentic was. It's taken several years, lots of learning, failed attempts, masks off and on, precious understanding, self-compassion, and faith, but I'm finally living and being true to myself. Fast-forward and I'm intent on being my authentic self.

What does it take to be authentic?

In my experience, there are a few things that come in handy when working toward being authentic. The very first thing and the most important is letting go of that falsely derived self-concept in order to get busy developing self-awareness. Knowing who you are in your heart is the most important part of being real. Self-awareness is what happens when you take a good look at yourself, literally and figuratively. Diving deep into understanding what matters to you, where your talents lie, what truths you hold dear, and how you want to be in the world is what it takes. Fortunately, at this point you've worked on exploring these characteristics and should have a really good baseline of knowing yourself at least a little bit better. It's also good to be aware of who or what may be influencing you or making you think you need to be a certain way or on a certain path. While others mean well, the guidance they give is based on what they value or believe—which may not necessarily align with what matters to you or to the path you're on. We talked about this with regards to perfection, but our battle with peer pressure or family pressure is a real deal when it comes to being ourselves. Awareness of all we're up against is just the beginning.

You must be resolute. Andie Walsh stays true to herself throughout her high school journey in *Pretty in Pink*. She opens herself up to new experiences, but always remains in tune with her gut instincts and finds strength in her true self. Being resolute didn't mean she didn't still feel the fear, hurt, and outright pain. It meant that in spite of it, she was able to hold tight to everything that defined her in order to find the safety and strength to be courageous to the core. Being the real you takes courage and belief in yourself. When you embrace your uniqueness, those things that make you special, a stand-up, knock-down, drag-out hit, your self-esteem will grow and help you face your fear to be vulnerable with others. For this to happen, you must be honest. I love this quote from Andrew in *The Breakfast Club*: "We're all pretty bizarre. Some of us are just better at hiding it, that's all."[29] We need to stop hiding, remove our masks, and use this moment to be honest about who we are.

Showing who you really are to others creates trust, garners respect, and helps us build deeply connected relationships. That alone will feed our human desire and need for belonging. There's also another facet to authentic honesty that I should mention. It's important we own our mistakes and take responsibility for our actions. That's a big one, so let that sink in a moment. We need to be this honest with ourselves and others to strengthen our integrity. Having integrity is what it means to live in authenticity. Not only do we need to be truthful, but we need to say what we mean and mean what we say; we need to face situations and others with no judgment; we need to use positive self-talk; above all we need to approach everything with kindness and love. It's time to speak your truth and share your thoughts and ideas, while also being mindful and respectful of others.

Let me share another story that might help put this all into perspective. When I turned 50, I also found myself living in a new climate. One that meant I would often be in a bathing suit. Yep, I moved to the beach. I know, you're thinking, "What in the world does this have to do with being authentic?" Bear with me as I set this up. I had the standard issue Mom-tankini, of course, but I also had a major issue with judging others. I realized I was spending my time at the beach or pool spiraling out thinking about why someone would wear a certain suit or why they thought they could get away with a bikini. Harsh, I know. I wasn't sitting there enjoying the nature or the calming beach vibes. I was using my energy to cut other women down in my mind, all the while wearing a fake-ass smile on my face. Not cool and really super shitty of me. I'm being completely honest with you about who I was being even though it wasn't my best moment because full transparency and honesty are an important part of who I am now as my authentic self.

It wasn't too long before I was lying at the pool, giving myself a subconscious bitch-slap. I snapped out of it and began to ask questions like, What was I doing? Why did I feel the need to be so nasty to other women? After all, this was not the type of person I wanted to be, nor was it the real me. I took a huge step back into some major self-awareness work and noticed I had a pattern of cutting on people for how they looked. I also noticed that people in my sphere of influence had this character trait too, sometimes even turning it on me and people I loved. I had to do something to change this behavior and find the real me in all of this negativity. I started peeling back the onion of my being to get to the root cause of this unwanted behavior. I was reminded of a moment in time where my attitude had shifted from being a loving and accepting person into a negative judgmental beast. At one of my lowest points in my life, intent on hiding my depression and unhappiness. I was masking my emotions around worthiness and enough-ness. I hide behind excess behaviors like emotional eating, smoking, being the whole party, and shifting the uncomfortable attention onto others by joking and laughing about how they looked. Anything to keep people from seeing me and my pain. This unwanted behavior solidified as I spent more and more time with these so-called friends, who modeled this negative behavior and I was picking it up. I never noticed what an impact being in and around that type of negative energy really had on me. I picked that gross skill up quickly and repeated that behavior for years.

Honestly, I am not proud of that time in my life, but it happened, and that was the root of this nasty mask I was wearing. Once I put all of this together, I knew my why. I had been struggling with my own negative body image, my self-worth and self-concept. I turned my internal judgment onto others because of my inadequacy. This had gone on far too long, and I knew I had to get straight about who I was and why I felt the need to be so unkind and negative. I jumped feet-first into the deep end with some major work on my self image. I started to look at my body, really look, exploring every inch and experiencing every emotion. I soon realized I was still hiding for no good reason. This exercise had opened my mind to the beauty of our unique shapes and sizes. I ran out and bought my first bikini in 25 years and put it on. I walked right out to the beach and stood there completely uneasy, vulnerable, and without a single care for anyone else because I was so exposed emotionally, mentally, and physically. I made myself show up in real life as the real me, no longer hiding behind the tankini safety net. I put myself out there for all to see, for me to see, for me to love and learn. The more I stepped out from behind my mask, the more my thoughts shifted and my brain began to rewire. I tapped into my authentic artist, remembering how the human form is intriguing, beautiful, and rich with form and function. I let loving kindness be my guide by focusing first on loving myself, viewing my body as a unique work of art. I used this approach to help me see the beauty in all forms, to redirect my thinking and shift from shame and judgment to open and loving appreciation. Every time I had a negative thought creep in, I quickly redirected it to my new perspective.

I tell you all of this because it's hard to own your shit and rewire your brain to be a better human, but tapping into your authentic self, your values, strengths, beliefs, and reason for being—it all helps support you and lovingly get you to a more positive place in life. Even writing this for you to read, I have a major lump in my throat. It's as real as I can be on this page and that is the entire point of this chapter. Having spent that last few years working on this one change, I've seen an incredible difference in myself and my interactions with others. Gone are the judgment, shame, and ridicule. I know it sounds unreal, but I'm now living in a space of acceptance and appreciation. I'm so grateful for this lesson and this humbling experience that has helped me become a better person.

Approaching life as your true self is a chance to change your perspective, like we've talked about before. The big issue is that human nature is to go along to get along, so we have to rewire our brain to view life from a new perspective. Looking at life from a new perspective like this, one where we don't have to adapt, a place where we can confidently be our best selves whatever that looks like, is the goal. It's about being true to yourself over being something you're not and figuring out who that person really is. The goal is to feel genuinely confident in your skin, safe to be yourself, living a life aligned with your true values, strengths, beliefs, and gifts. It doesn't mean you won't have hurts, worries, or fears—and it's not a license to be arrogant or rude. Being real comes from a place of peace, kindness, acceptance, and love.

Is authenticity worth the work?

Understanding, loving, and being your authentic self doesn't just happen overnight. Trust me, though, the moment you decide to be yourself an energetic shift occurs. It's worth the work! I feel as if Gen-X women time after time continue to keep ourselves small because we're all afraid that there isn't enough space in this world for our light to shine. Imagine what the space would look like if we all came out shining and rising up together. Not only is your light going to shine bright, but your well-being is sure to get an immediate jolt for the better. Being yourself alleviates a ton of stress, since you're no longer trying to fit in. You'll gain a serious boost to the self-esteem, increased happiness, unlimited potential, a sense of safety, self-respect, peace, and joy.

Our uniqueness can be crazy, exciting, and fun if we let it. Why not experience life in a new, open way—not being led by the crowd, but becoming and being true to yourself, finding yourself in a new way without restrictions, just being yourself? For this, you need to believe in yourself. Believing in yourself gives you the confidence needed to take action and get things done, so you can achieve greatness. Don't underestimate yourself. You have mad skills, and you are a force to be reckoned with. Say it with me... "I believe in myself!" After all, "Nobody puts Baby in a corner!"[30]

Quick, here's a couple of prompts to help you get started on being your true self:

• Take a moment each morning to actually look yourself in the mirror, really look, and say 3 nice things about the person you see.
• Fold a sheet of paper in half, and using one side, create a list of all the negative things you think about yourself. Flip the paper, and on the opposite side rewrite the negative as a positive statement.
• Write a letter to yourself, describing who you really are deep down in your core. Wait a week and read it to see if it describes the real you or needs more information. Continue to tweak the letter until it rings true.
• Pick one person each day this week to say something positive to. Smile and be the shining light you are.

Get a Grip

/get/ /ə,ā/ /grip/
idiom

1. phrase used to express the need to keep or recover one's self-control. Ex. *"Get a grip, lady!"*
2. to make an effort to control your emotions and behave more calmly. Ex. *"I think she ought to get a grip on herself."*

(me, myself, and i)

In order to get a grip, you have to take a beat and slow down. Easier said than done these days, but necessary nonetheless. In just the past few years, there has been so much chatter around self-care. So much so that it comes off as selfish to a generation such as ours, who were conditioned to spend all of our time putting more importance on hard work than taking care of ourselves.

It's time you stop pushing yourself to the max. Gone are the days of getting up at the crack of dawn to get in a killer workout only to jump into a full sprint of a day. If you're the typical Gen-X momma, you're half-dressed for work, cramming the kids in the car, shoving a breakfast bar down their throats, kicking them out the door at school, dropping the dog at the vet, and picking up the dry-cleaning all on the way to work. All the while you're burning the candle at both ends to get that big project completed for your nagging boss, facing down 300 unreturned emails, and stopping by the team-building happy hour before you're off to pick up the kids, fix dinner, and please your man (WTF? Thanks for this one, Mom). Quite frankly, who has the energy?

This is the moment you either have a complete mental breakdown or you decide to turn off the fire hose and take a beat. Time to stretch your legs and beg the question... What about you? Who's caring for you?

I believe I can speak for all of the women of Generation X when I say we were never taught to prioritize ourselves. At least, this was true for me. My mom never taught me anything about how important it is to take care of yourself throughout all the other demands life throws at you. In fact, I don't think she knew to share her experience or how badly we as women need the refresh, let alone tell me how to do it or name it self-care. If you're one of the lucky ones and were taught this magical skill, well, feel free to skip this one and move along. For the rest of us, we're gonna need a tutorial.

We're going to walk through this one slowly. It will take everything you have to keep from jumping right back into the familiar crazy that is life. To really start caring for yourself, you'll need to learn to settle into a new, calmer, slower state of being and find your inner motivation—the one that will navigate you more intentionally through all the chaos.

What's with the Self?

It's always good to explore the origin of urban legends, like self-care, to get a better understanding of what we're actually dealing with. I heard the self explained in a magical way years ago by Ekhart Tolle. He said, "You as the consciousness is the self."[31] I took this to mean that the self is your essence, your inner light, something that can not be seen, touched, or identified, Your being. On a spiritual level, it is transcendent. It's your energy, your vibration, beyond space and understanding. It's such a beautiful thought to behold. The self, our inner being, demands to be cared for in every facet. This is why it has taken on a life of its own with our current zeitgeist. We're not going to get into all of the psychology behind the self with the ego and the meaning attached to the different determinations; that is for another time. However, we will get into the total and complete bombardment of the term, self.

There are so many "selfs" these days that it's hard to know where to begin. We have been blessed with terms like self-concept, self-awareness, self-compassion, self-esteem, self-respect, self-discovery, self-image, self-efficacy, self-love, self-development, self-actualization, self-worth, self-control, self-talk, self-reflection, self-assured, self-made, self-help... You get the picture. The problem is that something so vast as the self cannot be compartmentalized, although we try as we might to break it down into bite-sized pieces.

Our most popular, all-encompassing term is self-care. Before we dive into how we can use self-care for good, we need to understand what it's not. This little honey has sent us all into a collective tizzy with its unrealistic and privileged expectations. It's become this badge of honor and a mechanism for shaming that is counter-intuitive to the entire purpose for the term in the first place. It can make you feel pretty lousy if you're thinking everybody else is able to have spa days, elaborate self-care rituals, or a self-actualized, "leveled-up" pampered existence, and you're not. You've been on social media. You've seen the how-to videos and thought-provoking posts of every influencer and celebrity you can name. They're spending all their time and energy telling you just how you should do self-care. From taking milk baths to weekends in St Bart's with the gang, they're all sharing the best products, locations, and rituals. All this noise is giving me a headache.

However, caring for yourself doesn't always look this way. In fact, it can be so remedial that you don't even know you're doing it. Although social media makes it look luxurious, which would be fun, the reality is that most of us can't even afford the time and energy to take a bath, let alone jet off to an ashram for a retreat weekend micro-dosing mushrooms. Imagine a woman who's working 2 to 3 jobs to put food on the table with no help, just hoping that her children are getting a good education and the proper nutrition to get through their day. Why should that woman feel pressured to change her schedule in order to meditate or go to puppy yoga? We are missing the point of the caring.

Obviously, there is a definite difference in what we each experience in life, even in how we care for ourselves. The problem comes in because we are a society bent on making self-care a competition instead of a normal part of everyone's daily lives. If we are going to normalize intentionally caring for ourselves, we have to approach collectively with loving support and admiration. In order to do this, we're going to need to stop making such a big deal out of it. Stop patting ourselves on the back and saying how great it is that we did this magical self-care experience today. We have to change our perspective and approach to caring for ourselves. Making it less of a thing and more of a way of being (for our inner being). If we come together as a community and acknowledge that not all women have access to the same things, we can begin to openly have a conversation about what real care could look like.

The goal in bringing all of this up is to be transparent and honest about how something so good can also cause so much shame and anguish. My hope is to change the perspective that caring for yourself is selfish and encourage you to make changes where you can. There are always two sides to every coin, and it's good to be mindful of how both sides look.

Where and how do we begin to nourish and care for ourselves?

We women are so very good at giving a ton of time and energy to everything and everyone else, but we never really replenish and take anything for ourselves. It's hard, because when you're making the time to care for yourself, you have to choose to remove something else from the priority list.

If you are ready to make yourself a priority, you can start caring for yourself by allowing yourself the time to access choice and change. For this to happen you have to have the means to have a choice and the ability to make a change. Therefore, you'll need to be clear on what you're working with—your circumstance and ability. Once again, this takes having greater awareness.

Awareness is and has been integral to our journey thus far and is the best place to begin. This is a big nugget, and that's why it's first. Awareness is such an important place to start, especially when it comes to caring for yourself. You not only need to know who you are and what you want your life to be like, but you also need to know your circumstance and what you can allow yourself to change in order to make your care a priority. You can be so busy in your daily life that the last person you even think about is yourself. Women can be like that, especially our generation. An even bigger issue is where and how we even choose to begin with every celebrity, influencer, author, and guru selling their own brand of self-care.

Let's take a moment. Step outside of yourself and away from all of the swirling going on around you right now. Look in the mirror and ask yourself, "What do I need right now to make me feel _____?" You know what you're experiencing, so I'm confident you can fill in the blank here. If not, just add the word "ME" and move along. This simple act of self-awareness might be just the care you need. I mean, how often do you have someone look you in the face and ask you what you need?

As an example, you want to feel calm; and in order for that to happen, you'd love to be able to take a long hot bath. The next thing you need to figure out is what's stopping you from getting that relaxing bath. Time for more fill in the blanks. "If I want to take a long hot bath, I would have to stop doing _____." This is where shift happens.

When you know how you feel and how you want to feel, coupled with how you can make that happen, then you can make informed decisions about how to get yourself there. Just as with any situation, the more you know and the more you envision improving, the easier it will be to make a decision and have a different experience. For instance, if you could get in a long hot bath by not fixing dinner, then maybe you order a pizza. While you wait for that pizza, you get to have your bath. It could be that easy or not, but you get the picture of why it's important to be aware of all the things. After all, caring for yourself is about choices and changes. Two things depend on knowing more. Beyond awareness, prioritizing our care also needs proper nourishment and subsequent care.

We can break this entire care nugget into three areas of concentration, each just as important as the other and imperative if we are going to make ourselves a priority. This trifecta is going to help us obtain holistic health, healing, and a better life.

The first of our steps is to truly tend to your needs. This is going to look different for everyone, but the general point is to nourish and protect yourself. Tending is caring for yourself, but it's also nurturing. Tending to your needs means giving yourself actual nourishment through food, water, movement, proper rest, connecting with others, learning and having new experiences—everything we talked about and more. It also means protecting yourself through setting boundaries, resetting expectations, looking at life with a new perspective and positive light.

You already have the basics down pat. Each day when you get out of bed, you brush your teeth. More than a habit, brushing your teeth is something you do, mostly on auto-pilot, without a thought. This behavior is ingrained into your life. It's a part of you. We're going one step further than the basics by nourishing, protecting, and cultivating the life you want, so it becomes a natural reaction, a routine fixture, a part of the internal conversation that you have with yourself each day. Really caring for yourself means you're actively working to improve your health and well-being by more than just the physical. Remember, it's about nourishing your spirit, your emotions, your brain, your relationships, your career, absolutely everything including your body. To do this you have to prioritize finding harmony, health, and contentment in all areas of your life.

Don't forget there is also the protection piece to support. This comes into play when we set realistic boundaries. Saying no is the ultimate act of caring for yourself. I've said it before and I'll say it again, when you protect what's important to you, it will remain the priority. Having defined limits will keep you from continuing to fill your cup with things that no longer serve you. Setting boundaries will set you free and protect you. Give yourself the permission to set boundaries and stand by them, so you can have the time to reset, pivot, and navigate forward. It's a simple and healthy place to be. I love the fact that this level of care is at our fingertips and always within us.

Our second piece of the puzzle is to speak kindly about yourself. Self-talk is important because positive reinforcement from within builds confidence and strength and empowers you. Negative self-talk does the exact opposite. You can tear yourself down just as fast as you can build yourself up. How we talk to ourselves matters. The great thing is that if a negative thought creeps in, we have the ability to catch it and flip that statement around into a positive thought. It's simple, but it's still the magic that is the mind. Speaking to yourself from a place of love and kindness will instantly change how you're feeling for the better. It can be encouraging to hear yourself saying uplifting statements that boost yourself up and get you ready to take on the world. Whether it's perfection, perspective, authenticity, stress, or menopause, any and all of the things we've been dealing with as Gen-X women will take a little sweet talking. Caring for yourself and making your life better takes being optimistic and talking to yourself with love.

If you're not really ready to jump all in on blowing sweet nothings in your own ear, you can always use affirmations. Affirmations are another way you can focus in on calling yourself amazing to help you shift negative thoughts, calm your mind, and focus in on your goals and visions. I can't tell you how affirmations have helped my life without talking about my moment of chronic stress and burnout. As part of my healing journey, I used affirmations to get my head back on straight and to show myself how much I was loved—by me. I started by making a list of all the negative things I thought about myself; then just like I showed you in the prompts from the last chapter, I rewrote each statement as a positive. These became my affirmations. They help me retrain my brain and begin to see the world, myself, and my life in a positive light. It became a type of meditation, a morning ritual of healing and love.

The more you can talk to yourself with love and kindness, the better. You can enhance this by surrounding yourself with positive people and energy. There's nothing like having a crowd of cheerleaders reinforcing the message that you're a freakin' amazing human being. Positive vibes will do wonders for the soul, the mind, and the body.

The last but not the least of the ways to care is by having compassion for yourself. This is where you get to learn and share a little grace with yourself. We've already talked about how self-compassion is the ultimate gift when relieving stress, but it's also the ultimate in really caring for yourself. It not only relieves stress, but it allows you to heal, be more mindful, safely process your emotions, regulate your nervous system, and makes us feel happy, calm, and less anxious.

Showing ourselves grace and compassion is a coping mechanism we would all do well to embrace. Compassion doesn't come with shame, guilt, or fear. It's filled with love, understanding, kindness, empathy, sensitivity, and a little bit of tender loving care. Who couldn't use more of that on the daily? How you talk to yourself, how you treat yourself, the compassion you show for yourself, how you spend your time day to day—all are important to your eternal health and happiness.

What can making yourself a priority look like?

This is where we all need to realize self-care could be something so simple. Something that touches your soul or your inner being. It doesn't have to cost you any money, maybe just the time it takes for a moment to breathe, read a motivational quote someone sent you, have a conversation with a friend or with your child. Maybe that's a good place to begin. Keep it simple, stupid!

Self-care is...

Finding a way to manage your stress,

A deep breath between meetings,

Looking in the mirror and saying, "I love you!"

It's all this and so much more.

Prioritizing yourself can look like anything and everything that supports your nourishment, protection, perspective, and compassion. The beauty of it is that you can care for yourself at home, just as easy as you would by going on a retreat or otherwise leaving the house. It really can happen anywhere, anytime, and anyhow you'd like. While we can't control everything the world sends our way, we can dictate the ideal situation for how we handle our healing. Tapping into all of the skills you've learned so far will help you approach how you care for yourself with mindful intention.

My mom recently told me that she would occasionally swap babysitting with a friend, in order to have a day off from taking care of me and my sisters. What a relief that must have been for her to take the day, but also hard because she had to ask someone to watch us and trust that they would take just as good of care with us as she would. She did it and said it was the most refreshing and rewarding thing she could have done for herself and for us. Shame she never told me about that or the importance of it before I made it to midlife all fried; but I know now, and I'm having it different.

If you need support in making yourself a priority, turn to your community. Your community can help you slow down and pace yourself, taking some of the pressure off by doing something like watching your kids. Mommy and Me is a perfect example of how your community can relieve some of the burden in order for you to focus on relaxing the pace of your day. Asking for help is a great avenue for slowing down and prioritizing yourself by delegating tasks that are forcing you to fast-track your day. Whether you access your community or go it solo, you can make prioritizing your self all your own.

I've been purposely building a life full of self-care moments and milestones. As a burnout survivor, I knew what happened when I didn't take care of myself. What I came to realize in my healing was the importance of properly caring for myself. As I began to redesign my life, I made a point to prioritize myself, my health, and my well-being above all else. In order to do this I had to design a life full of enriching moments and solid habits to support me in every way possible. I was fortunate enough to have a loving partner who walked alongside me in making these changes—a complete privilege and a godsend. I not only changed my life, but our family as a whole changed dramatically for the better. My breakdown was a blessing— and even more than that, it was the catalyst to a complete, total, and life-changing breakthrough.

I gained tremendous perspective around who I was (my authentic self) and the life I wanted to live (my vision), through soul-searching, research, and therapeutic exploration. I took a pause, a slowdown if you will, and decided that I didn't want to wake up with an alarm anymore. I wanted to ease into my day and not open a computer for at least the first 2 hours. I wanted to be in a place that inspired me and connected me with nature. I needed to be surrounded by loving family and friends, who let me create meals and curate experiences for them. I wanted my life to be filled with love—and more than anything, I wanted to feel like I was contributing to the greater good.

My life evolved into a manifestation of personal care, nourishment, protection, and love. The one takeaway here that might be the most impactful for you is the importance of slowing down.

What do you mean by "slow down"?

Slowing down allows us to see the opportunities and the potential we have with regards to ourselves and our lives. Slowing down is the ultimate act of self-care. It is the opportunity to heal at a pace that our mind, body, and soul understand. We've all become accustomed to the rush, the constant business, the rat-race pace that has us continually in a reactive state of mind. When we try to slow down, it feels uncomfortable and has us on edge, because we are used to going full-tilt. Life in the fast lane, if you want to get all Don Henley about it. If you dare to embrace it, slowing down will be the single most impactful act of self-care you'll ever take.

Take a moment to... slow your roll. This is going to look very different for many of us for all the reasons we're previously discussed. Picture, if you will, sitting at the dinner table eating mindfully, enjoying every bite, along with a little light dinner conversation with the family. Go slow. Take a moment for a deep breath in the elevator or a walk alone around the block. Go slow. Really listen to your body and hear what it's trying to tell you. Go slow. Shut off your phone (I know this one is triggering, but stay with me) and take an intentional technology break while you watch a movie with your kids. Go slow. Laugh with friends, listen to the sounds of nature, take an entire afternoon off, whatever it looks like for you just go at a slower pace.

Slowing down doesn't have to be a big act of cultural defiance to be impactful. It can be as easy as breathing. Make a choice to give yourself permission to choose to slow down. If we can't slow down, then we can't heal, and then we're no good to ourselves or anyone for that matter. We women are designed to nurture and care; we just need to turn that natural instinct toward how we treat ourselves.

Learning to care for yourself, like life, will continue to evolve and iterate. As you reach each new level, you gain wisdom, experience more things, and you continue to grow. In my path to taking care of myself, I've begun to look at self-care differently. I recently asked myself: What if, instead of the term self-care, we started to use the word kindness? What if we called it a kindness day, instead of a self-care day? Have a kindness ritual, instead of a self-care ritual. Show yourself some kindness, instead of showing yourself some care. Just changing that one word raises the vibration and moves it away from this "thing" we have to do into a way of being. Would you rather do self-care or be kind? Try it on for size and maybe, just maybe, we can start a kindness movement instead of a self-care movement.

Why do we need to care for ourselves?

Caring for yourself means you'll tap into greater awareness, you'll be able to give more, have higher self-esteem, and feel empowered—but also increase productivity, possibly lose weight, and basically improve your overall health and well-being. It's time for an intentional slowdown to redirect your efforts, take back your time and energy, and put it to better use taking care of your me, myself, and I.

Studies have shown that if we are healthy, our state of being reverberates out, and the collective "WE" becomes healthy. Making sure that you are eating good food transcends into your family eating good food. Making sure you are hydrated teaches your coworkers how to stay hydrated. Asking your friends to go along on your morning walk extends to them having moved more in their day.

Let's work on supporting each other to remove the unrealistic bar we've set to achieve more and set our needs aside. If we collectively normalize nestling into our uniqueness and prioritize caring for ourselves, we will become the something we do every day to live in a better state of mind and being. It is necessary to slow down and care for yourself. Therefore, we need to reverse the notion that self-care is a goal or another task, a ritualistic thing we hold up on a pedestal. It's not a pie-in-the-sky, unattainable thing, and obsessing over it doesn't help us at all. If we change our perspective and approach, we can pivot away from cultivating a society that celebrates the woman who can juggle it all and create a community that allows people to be who they are and be kind to themselves first and foremost.

Here are a few thoughts on how you can get started being kind to yourself:

• Right now, wherever you're seated, take a moment to adjust your posture. Sit up straight, throw those shoulders back and down, chest out, stomach in, sitting as though you have a straight line from the top of your head to the middle of your hip bones.
• Each morning this week, look at yourself in the mirror and say, "I am my priority!"
• Give yourself permission to take a 20-minute break to sit, walk, pray, or just be outside. Pro tip: Leave the phone inside.

Bummer

/ˈbʌmər/
noun

1. A disappointing or unpleasant situation.
Ex. *"It's a real bummer that she can't get out of her own way."*

(you will persevere)

Even with the best laid plans, the Gen-X woman knows things get in the way, life gets messy, and roadblocks pop up. It can be a total bummer when we get stuck in a space of over-analyzing so much that we create imaginary roadblocks as to why we just can't move forward. We may even tack on a bit of anxiety around that step forward just to sweeten the deal. Whatever blocks you from taking a step forward, please know that we all struggle with getting out of our own way at times. Whatever it takes for you to move forward is what it takes. Sometimes that's a total shift from how you thought you were going to get there, and that's okay.

Even after reading everything I've unwrapped in this book, you still might be struggling with that first step. This could be for many reasons, so let's explore some of the possible obstacles that may be getting in your way.

We just talked about negative self-talk being a huge deterrent in not only your self-concept, but also in your health. You might be saying, "I can't," or, "It's never going to work for me," or my favorite—"I don't have enough time." If you're proclaiming your defeat before you've even begun, then the chances of you moving past the obstacle are slim to none. Negative self-talk keeps you from reaching your full potential. It actually keeps you from even seeing the opportunities to reach that potential. This pessimistic attitude and negative nurturing are detrimental to your mental health, not to mention moving forward. Talking down to yourself in a bad or limiting way can cause you feelings of despair, depression, loneliness, sadness, and stress—which in turn can also lower your immune function, raise your blood pressure, disrupt your hormone balance, and distort your thinking.

Another major obstacle is Impostor Syndrome. This is a relatively new term, but a long-time struggle and obstacle for Gen-X women, like me. No matter the situation or the reason, we have spent years not believing that we should be as successful as we're capable of. Let that sink in a moment if you will. Even if you were to succeed, you're questioning whether its legitimate or not. What a messed-up and twisted perspective to have. Talk about getting in your own way. This might just be the granddaddy of all negative self-talk. Unfortunately, it pops up time and time again as we spiral with self-doubt.

That self-doubt creeps in as we come up against the obstacle and idea of perfection. As we discussed before, we've been conditioned to strive for the mythical goal of being perfect. As you try to rewire your thoughts on perfection, the pressure of cultural norms and well-meaning friends and family can be a constant roadblock. Shifting to a more authentic existence doesn't come without the threat of falling back into familiar worthiness issues: low self-esteem, depression, anxiety, and so much more. It's such a highly toxic situation for you, mentally and emotionally, that it requires some heavy lifting.

Part of the work around breaking the notion of perfection is another obstacle. "They" are all well-meaning and have a different perspective on who and how you should be. I'm talking about the others in your life who pressure you with expectations that might not align with who you're becoming or where you're headed. This can be a hard obstacle, because we love our friends and family and understand they mean well. We don't want to be rude or hurt their feelings, but having the conversation or changing the way we view those constructive moments of criticism takes strength, work, and tighter boundaries.

Losing hold of those boundaries can also be a challenge and create obstacles to moving the needle in your life. In writing this book, I've made and lost my boundaries with others with regards to my time and commitment to my business and partnerships, as well as struggling with my own creative schedule. Boundaries are only as strong as we keep them and often get bulldozed even though we have the best of intentions. This often affects our time.

Time is a valuable resource that is NOT renewable. It was my nemesis and my excuse for decades. Because time is fleeting, we try to hold on to it for dear life in a world full of time sucks. I don't know how much time I've lost in a doom scroll on social media or with my previous corporate schedule of 5+ meetings a day. Time however is not the enemy, but it can be a stressor.

Which leads us to stress. What an incredible obstacle to be overcome. Thank goodness we explored managing stress within chapter 2. The unfortunate thing is that there will always be stress, good and bad. Life just exists with it, so having it rear its ugly head and block your path toward a greater existence is inevitable. You'll find that stress comes at you in all shapes and sizes, but one we most often feel is financial stress.

Money is an obstacle for most of us, and for good reason. Everything costs something or has a dollar amount that defines its value. Even time is money. It's a stressor because sometimes we struggle to meet our basic needs let alone our wants without money. Lack of money can keep us from accessing resources needed to move forward with our vision. It's a big challenge that may be a result of lack of financial knowledge, a burden of a large unplanned expense, or something that resonates with most women, a wage gap. Which leads us right into your last major obstacle—your job.

If I had a dime for every time my previous employment got in the way of my life, I wouldn't have to write this book. No, seriously, it may be the reason why each of these other obstacles exist. Think about it. Negative self-talk, impostor syndrome, perfectionist drive, losing hold of your boundaries, lack of time, lack of money, freaking stress—all are a direct result of work. This necessity gets in our way time and time again. It is the one we place the most blame upon, but also the one we allow to block our momentum.

I'm sure this all sounds totally doom and gloom, but the truth is life happens. Inevitably you will get distracted from what you're working toward. All of these obstacles could be potential blocks you'll encounter along the way. **So how can we be the eye of the tiger, rise up to the challenge of our rivals, and survive?**[32]

It begins with gratitude. It's not that often that we really take a moment to appreciate the good in our lives, or the wonder and awe of all the majesty around us, even in the face of adversity. Expressing gratitude is more than just a "Thank You." It's having a deep sense of appreciation and awe at the little things that enrich your life.

Let's do a little exercise. Stop what you're doing right now and close your eyes (well, read this first and then close your eyes). Take this time to think about one person, place, or thing you're grateful for. I know it sounds corny, but you can do it. Alright, are you thinking about it? As you sit here with your eyes closed, thinking about that one thing that has enriched your life, begin to think about the details. The location, the weather, the sounds, the smells, anything and all you can remember. Let your senses remember your experience and become part of why you appreciate it so much. As you sit in this attitude of gratitude, begin to notice how your body is responding. Are you feeling warmth in your face? Do you have a smile? Did your shoulders drop? Are you feeling the tension in your body melt away? Has your breathing slowed or deepened? Are you relaxed? Make note of how appreciating one little thing in your big life has made your body and mind feel in this moment. Alright you can open your eyes. The trick here is to turn to gratitude when you feel like you just can't deal with what life is throwing at you.

One thing is for sure, gratitude ripples like a pebble thrown into the water. Practicing gratitude has been found to give a boost to the immune system, improve sleep, brighten your mood, reduce chronic pain and risk of disease, lower blood pressure, alleviate stress, and slow down the aging process. And that's just physical. It raises your self-esteem, gives you a sense of connection, boosts your mood, and makes you happy, more empathetic, and compassionate. If there was a pill you could take that would give you all of this, you'd take it, right? Well, the prescription here is a daily dose of gratitude. Bonus for you: The side effect is being able to see all of the areas in your life that are abundant.

What else can you do when life shifts, your good intentions slide, and your progress stales out? A survival plan might be just what the doctor ordered. When life gets you down and there is no motivation, you need a solid support plan to calm, focus, rejuvenate, reset, and reinforce your efforts. What could be better than the best Gen-X movies, music, food, fun for building a plan to get you back on track, overcome obstacles, and persevere with grace? For all those moments you find yourself in need of a little comfort and support, I give you your personal **Gen-X Survival Guide**. You'll notice there are several spaces still open. This is on purpose so you can insert your favorite go-tos. Remember these are meant to be spaces for the things you can turn to when you fall off the horse and need comfort, motivation, or support. Now, get in there and add your personal touch.

Movies are emotions in action enabling you to step out of your reality and see the bigger picture.
1) Feel Good | *Ferris Bueller's Day Off* (1986)
2) Empowerment | *Nine to Five* (1980) or *Working Girl* (1988)
3) Inspiration | *Goonies* (1985)
4) _____
5) _____
6) _____

Music will reconnect you to the inner you.
1) Motivation | "Groove is in the Heart" - Deee-Lite (1990)
2) Energy | "Pump Up the Jam" - Technotronic (1989)
3) Nostalgia | "It's Tricky" - Run-D.M.C. (1986)
4) _____
5) _____
6) _____

Fun will help you focus and slow down a moment to get reset.
1) Putt-Putt for the fun of it
2) Cruising main street (Don't forget to circle through the

McDonald's parking lot)
   3)   Ride bikes with a gang of friends
   4)   _____
   5)   _____
   6)   _____

Food
   1)   Hostess Snacks (of any kind—I'm partial to Ding Dongs, but
strictly for comfort on a special occasion)
   2)   Spinach artichoke dip in a bread bowl
   3)   Jell-O Jigglers
   4)   _____
   5)   _____
   6)   _____

There are a couple other categories you need to build out, in order to
round out your survival guide. You'll need your **Homegirls**. I know
you've already identified those ladies who you can call on in your
moment of need, and they will come in really handy when life throws
you a curve ball. There are a couple lines here, but feel free to add
more to the list.

   1)   _____
   2)   _____
   3)   _____

The last thing you need is a little **geography**. An important part
of your survival guide is location, location, location. As we've talked
about before, your environment has a huge impact on your state of
mind. Take a moment and list places where you can go to calm your
soul, ignite your creativity, or restore your spirit.

   1)   _____
   2)   _____
   3)   _____

Once you have your survival guide complete, you'll have a fullproof plan to squash any obstacles and crush any roadblocks that get in your way.

Just in case you need extra support, feel free to reference this poem for the strength and motivation to move forward.

When God created woman he was working late on the 6th day.
An angel came by and asked, "Why spend so much time on her?"
The Lord answered, "Have you seen all the specifications I have to meet to shape her?

She must function in all kinds of situations.
She must be able to embrace several kids at the same time.
Have a hug that can heal anything from a bruised knee to a broken heart.
She must do all this with only two hands.
She cures herself when sick and can work 18 hours a day."

The angel was impressed, "Just two hands...impossible!
And this is the standard model?"
The angel came closer and touched the woman.
"But you have made her so soft, Lord."
"She is soft," said the Lord,
"But I have made her strong. You can't imagine what she can endure and overcome."

"Can she think?" The angel asked.
The Lord answered, "Not only can she think, she can reason and negotiate."
The angel touched her cheeks.
"Lord, it seems this creation is leaking! You have put too many burdens on her."
"She is not leaking...it is a tear." the Lord corrected the angel.
"What's it for?" Asked the angel.
The Lord said, "Tears are her way of expressing her grief, her doubts, her love, her loneliness, her suffering and her pride."

This made a big impression on the angel,
"Lord, you are a genius. You thought of everything. A woman is indeed
marvelous!"
The Lord said, "Indeed she is.

She has strength that amazes a man.
She can handle trouble and carry heavy burdens.
She holds happiness, love and opinions.
She smiles when she feels like screaming.
She sings when she feels like crying.
Cries when happy and laughs when afraid.
She fights for what she believes in.
Her love is unconditional.
Her heart is broken when a next-of-kin or a friend dies but she finds
strength to get on with life."

The angel asked: "So she is a perfect being?"
The Lord replied, "No. She has just one drawback...she often forgets
what she is worth."

One last thing, use these prompts to help you persevere:

• Pick up some nostalgic candy on your way out of the grocery store to create an emergency survival kit
• Put on one of your old concert T-shirts and turn up the tunes
• When you're faced with a challenge this week, stop what you're doing and take a moment to think about one thing you are grateful for
• Don't give up—you have a plan; use it

Groovy

/ˈɡruː.vi/
adjective

1. very fashionable and interesting.
Ex. "That's a groovy hat you're wearing."
2. marvelous. wonderful. excellent.
Ex. "I'm feeling groovy."

(being in the flow)

By this point, you've had quite the journey of self-discovery. You've learned more about yourself, you know your worth, you're embracing your authenticity, celebrating your imperfections, and allowing your inner beauty to shine. We've rallied together so you can make real changes happen. With a better understanding of what aging and midlife are and are not, it's time to let your dynamic energy flow. Throughout this entire book, you've been gaining a better understanding of what it will takes to rise up, redefine, rewrite, and reset what it means to live, in spite of the hand you've been dealt as a Gen-X woman.

So what's next?

The truth is that when you're doing the work and moving forward, you'll ultimately work your hardest and do your best. At the same time, it can also rob you of joy, especially when you expect things to come more easily than they do or you're so hyper-focused that you aren't present enough to enjoy the ride. All this work comes down to living in the groovy state of mind that is the FLOW. I know your mom never told you about this, because not too many people today even talk about what it looks like to flow through life. You've probably heard the more popular buzzwords like thrive, strive, level up, flourish, or others, but they are all about working toward something or maintaining a vibe—and we're past that at this point.

The flow is a state of being. Like Yoda says in *The Empire Strikes Back*, "Do or do not, there is no try."[33] It's living true to yourself, your values, your beliefs, your purpose, your vision, just letting it all flow without struggle, striving, or worry. The flow is a result of your personal journey and is the ultimate state of well-being. When YOU find harmony and health in all areas of YOUR life, you're in the flow. Don't get me wrong, there will be ups and downs with the good, bad, and ugly days, but they will all be more manageable and supported as you flow.

What does it take to flow?

When I began to heal from my burnout, I received real clarity around who I was as my authentic self and what my purpose at that moment needed to be. Once I set my sights on becoming a certified health and wellness coach, everything just fell into place. It sounds crazy, but the moment I wrote down in my journal, "the world's health coach," things just unfolded in front of me. Within the first six months of my journey, I earned two of my five certifications, left my corporate burnout job, lost thirty pounds, made the decision to open my company, and began researching new cities for a cross-country move with my husband. Don't get me wrong, it took work, but it wasn't a struggle. One opportunity after another just opened in front of me. Each step I took to grow and evolve was met with blessing after blessing. It was an eye-opening experience that taught me what it took and looked like to be in the flow.

There are a couple things that need to happen in order to get yourself in the groove of the flow. They are acceptance, gratitude, and acceptance.

What is acceptance?

This is what happens when your life aligns fully with your values and beliefs. Acceptance is key to a fulfilled life. It means you're living without judgment and totally immersed in a healthy existence. Accepting who you are means you've created a life where you can stop judging yourself for those days when you just need an eclair. One where you can stop waiting for the "perfect" time and be brave enough to feel excited about your life again. I love what the character Brain Johnson wrote to Mr. Vernon from *The Breakfast Club* about acceptance.[34]

Dear Mr. Vernon, we accept the fact that we had to sacrifice a whole Saturday in detention for whatever it was we did wrong. But we think you're crazy to make us write an essay telling you who we think we are. You see us as you want to see us—in the simplest terms, in the most convenient definitions. But what we found out is that each one of us is a brain...and an athlete...and a basket case...a princess...and a criminal. Does that answer your question?
Sincerely yours, the Breakfast Club.

Accepting who you are and embracing your uniqueness will allow you to be present and embrace all life has to offer. Better yet, you'll be able to see the opportunities laying at your feet and hear your gut when it says to pick that up and run with it. You'll also need to tap into the mindfulness skills you've been working to develop.

So I have one big question... Are you present right now? Are you fully present in this moment and aware of where you are? What you're doing and how you're doing it? How are you impacting the people, space, and things around you?

There's no real judgment or action needed. You're just observing and being in the now. This is what it means to be mindful. As we've talked about before, mindfulness is crucial to our well-being. It creates a safe space for exploration, mental clarity, appreciation, and growth.

Mindfulness is one of the puzzle pieces needed to increase our gratitude and, in turn, our personal health.

Why do we need to be grateful?

Mindfulness may help you cultivate it, but gratitude is central to happiness. As you start paying more attention to your thoughts and looking for the good, you'll be able to appreciate all that you are and all that you have. Finding the joy and the pleasure in every moment is what the flow is all about. The more you recognize the good, you'll begin to see the glass as half full.

I read something that perfectly describes the relationship of gratitude and its importance to the experience of the flow posted by Melody Beattie from *The Language of Letting Go: Hazelden Meditation Series*.[35]

Gratitude unlocks the fullness of life. It turns what we have into enough, and more. It turns denial into acceptance, chaos to order, confusion to clarity. It can turn a meal into a feast, a house into a home, a stranger into a friend. It turns problems into gifts, failures into successes, the unexpected into perfect timing, and mistakes into important events. It can turn an existence into a real life, and disconnected situations into important and beneficial lessons. Gratitude makes sense of our past, brings peace for today, and creates a vision for tomorrow. Gratitude makes things right. Gratitude turns negative energy into positive energy. There is no situation or circumstance so small or large that it is not susceptible to gratitude's power. We can start with who we are and what we have today, apply gratitude, then let it work its magic.

Feeling gratitude gets you flowing, but a tangible practice of gratitude is needed for it to take hold of your life, so you can really reap the health+wellness benefits. I can honestly say I am more positive and mindful of where I am in my journey, living my life in the present. Instead of wanting and trying, I am now being and doing. It's definitely helped lower my stress and increase my happiness. I feel lighter and I continue to add more gratitude practices to my daily routine. I am reaping the benefits, but above all it has brought me joy and allowed me to experience, accept, and appreciate the flow.

I have a daily gratitude ritual, which I've been practicing for a while now.

• I schedule a monthly facial to show my skin some love and give myself some time to be offline.
• I do a daily meditation on insight timer usually in the morning and then I end the evening by listening to binaural beats.
• Most days I take a moment sometime around midday to write one thing I'm grateful for that day in my daily planner.
• I regularly set a daily intention. Most days it's just that I will live my life as a prime example of health and wellness as I'm walking the walk.

More recently, I've started re-framing how I talk about things I want, need, and envision for my life. I now talk about them in the present as if they are already happening. I started this practice after researching for a presentation I gave to a local ladies' organization. It came to me while reading some of Ekhart Tolle's work on gratitude and abundance. He basically said that if you are always in want or need, that it is counteractive to gratitude and attraction. Basically, the laws of attraction are at play.[36] So I changed my tone and approach immediately.

My gratitude practice didn't start with all of these steps happening at once. It was more of a ripple effect. After adding one thing, then I'd add the next when I felt I had formed a habit with the first step. I didn't want to overwhelm myself and stress out about having too much on my plate. This allowed me to really appreciate my life, to see everything I had and how amazing it was that I had so much.

Having a deep appreciation helps you really savor those good things and gives you the ability to absorb the joy and pleasure they give you. Deep appreciation is beyond words; it is an experience you have with embracing the good and feeling its effects on you. Better yet, this type of deep appreciation or gratitude breeds abundance.

When I read what Eckhart Tolle says here[37], it really spoke to me.

Acknowledging the good that you already have in your life is the foundation for all abundance.

I believe he's saying a life in gratitude is a life of abundance. Making the most of what we have turns it into more. Sometimes this is easier said than done, but it is in the difficult times where we need to take stock of what is good, what is working, where we are blessed. Our little friend awareness is the key to identifying all the ways life continually blesses you. It's my immediate go-to tool and probably yours by now. With gratitude, life becomes more clear giving us a whole new perspective. This grounded presence and perspective will enable you to then bend and flow with what comes your way, in complete contentment and joy. This is where satisfaction comes into the picture.

How can we feel satisfied?

Giving yourself permission to feel satisfaction may be a challenge too, but feeling satisfied with your life has its benefits. Being fully satisfied is the moment in which you fully accept yourself, are grateful, and find joy in your life.

This is when the sweet life feels sweet! All of the self-discovery and transition you've undergone as you've moved through this book was for one single intention—to feel more satisfied with your life. Along with satisfaction comes your inner peace, contentment, joy, and the all-too-popular happiness. What a full group this is. They gift us with a variety of physiological and psychological benefits too numerous to name, but they are a collective of all of the benefits we've talked about in each and every chapter of this book.

Being satisfied and enjoying the pleasure of life is what comes when your vision is actualized. Lucky for us, we'll create new visions and more moments to feel satisfaction as we grow into our true selves. I am currently on my third iteration of a vision for my life. Third, because I've actualized the other two and am satisfied with the outcome. It's an amazing place to be, and for this it is an important part of the flow. There is satisfaction in the flow and flow in the satisfaction. The two are intertwined and dependent on one another. When you're feeling the flow, it is groovy like a drive-in movie.

Once you get really moving on your vision, It's time to learn how to appreciate the life you are achieving and live it to its fullest. As they say in *Dead Poets Society*, "Carpe Diem, boys [ladies]. Seize the Day. Make your lives extraordinary!"[38]

How do you know when you're in the flow?

When I'm living true to my authentic self and in accordance with my purpose, everything seems to fall into place. I know it sounds arrogant and unrealistic, but I've experienced it; and now I use that feeling as my guide to knowing when I'm on the right path. I call it a message from God, but you may see it as a premonition or manifestation. Whatever it is to you, that feeling of life going your way—that's what the flow is all about.

I recently changed the direction of my company after much debate and introspection, which with no surprise to me (I'm used to it by now) was the most incredible example of flow. Things were stagnant and needed a reboot to meet the demands of our new market. It was a big stretch for me to roll out something that wasn't fully vetted or completely perfect (I'm a Virgo after all), but I took a leap of faith on a whim, and whoa! Things haven't stopped happening. They just keep rolling in and, quite frankly, I'm struggling to keep up with it all. I can feel the vibe. The energy is vibrating at an intensely high level, and I know I am on the right path. It's happening for a reason, partially because I got out of my own way, but also because it's God telling me that this is the path I was intended to be on with this business. It's so freaking punk rock, I can't stand it. I love being in the flow.

This is not about being Wonder Woman, because we know that's a myth. This is about being real and loving it. I hope you've enjoyed this complete guide to redefining how you age, taking your power back, determining fact from fiction, being fulfilled, feeling vibrant, and navigating all the nuances of midlife in order to have the beautiful life you deserve. If you remember nothing else, remember this, even in midlife, we Gen-X women are vital, vibrant, and important.

One very last set of prompts to help you enjoy the flow:

• Go forest bathing… Yep, a walk outside in nature has been shown to dramatically increase feelings of gratitude. Take a moment and stop to look around. Breathe in the air, tune into the sounds, smell the scents, and ground yourself by planting your feet in one place to really appreciate all that the universe has given. Be grateful for this moment and your environment. Be in awe and wonder at the majesty of life.
• Think of a moment when you felt completely in the groove. Marinate in that feeling and use that as a marker for how you want your flow to feel. Go back to it anytime you shift directions in your life, and if it doesn't match up, shift again.
• Try one of the gratitude practices from the outline in this chapter.
• Look yourself in the mirror and repeat after me, "I accept who I am. I am grateful for all that I have and all that I am. I am fully satisfied with ME!"
Now, say it again with conviction.

Shout Out

/SHout out/
noun

1. A message of congratulations, support, or appreciation.
Ex. *"It's time for a special shout out."*

(acknowledgments)

I'm not sure how I got here. This book was as much of a growth moment as any other in my crazy life. It challenged me to really assess my own life and the validity of sharing my journey, but also allowed me to be vulnerable and completely exposed (still processing). I used my life as a foundation of the book, but it was my conversations and experiences with the women I love in my life that really crafted the entire narrative. This book is a love letter to the tenacity and resilience of my beloved, often forgotten, generation of incredible women and those who know me best and still love me for it. I wouldn't be here if it wasn't for the many women in my life who've walked along side with me in sisterhood and love.

Although my mother and I don't always see eye to eye, as I reached the age of fifty, we began to share more stories, emotions, experiences in our conversations on and off air. Mom, I thank you for being my co-host and finally sharing those things you knew but never said until now. Because of you, I have realized midlife is easier when we women are vulnerable and share our truth.

My favorite friendships are those I share with my two amazing sisters, Julie and Emily. They are the reason I know what it means to really, truly, deeply love. The stubbornness, loud long laughs, crazy screaming matches, deep tears, pure bliss, boat drinks, and huge hugs have been a guiding force. This book is for them more than any other women, simply because I want them to live extremely long and happy lives by my side.

To my Wandas, Lisa and Helen, I say thank you for the honesty, snark, love, California-sobriety, inspiration, and lasting friendship. Near or far, we will always be there to cut a bitch or to put a little class in each other's glass.

To my CCIG ladies, Anne and Tiff, I am grateful for the investment in my life and our triple threat friendship. The Ville will never be the same without the three of us holding court and joining forces to take over the world. With you ladies by my side, anything is possible.

Lauren, you are my sister from another mister. Without your love, encouragement, unwavering friendship, and honesty, I would not be where I am today. You have been my compass and sidekick—for that I am forever grateful and in your debt.

To all of my dear friends in the Ville and Indy, I thank you for being there for me, sharing my highs and lows, helping me bury the bodies, clowning on co-workers, and holding my hair when I needed to literally and figuratively vomit. I couldn't have asked for more amazing friends, so let me give a few of you your flowers: Sue Moe, Sarah C., Peggy, Brette, Sarah H., Roxane, Papesh, my Pat Flynn's Sista's, Martha K., Diana, Whitney, Book Club, Card Club, Gene, Cookies, Mike K., Jeremy J., Jennifer L., Maggie S., Kathy H., Jill, Suzanne, Kathy S., Devin, KTap, Courtenay, Kellie A.(tits up), Melissa S., Beth M., and Chante. For all the other friends and family I cherish (IYKYK), I thank you for being a part of my life and helping me grow into my skin and beyond expectations.

I am incredibly thankful for my Rebeca Books family for seeing me, harnessing my potential, and trusting me enough to write this book. Without your encouragement and support none of this would be possible.

Certainly not the least, is how grateful I am for my husband, Travis. You bring me love, light, and so many laughs. I will always be eternally grateful to Whitney for texting me your photo and setting up our blind date. From that first moment you've listened with your good ear, embraced all of my bossy bits, and let me be authentically me. You are my moon and my stars. Sometimes I roll my eyes, but at least you're cute. My dad would have loved you.

Finally, to all who will read this book and allow me to be your guide in breaking the mold, I thank you above all and wish you all the hope and happiness in designing the life you long to live. Trust me... It is worth the work.

Your Homegirl

April Raque is out to change the perception of what it means to live a healthy life. She's creating a new consciousness—one where wellness is a practice and healthy aging is appealing, fun, stress-free, easy, and customizable. April is a Mayo Clinic Certified and National Board Certified Health and Wellness Coach (NBC-HWC), Reiki master, consultant, author, and co-host of the popular podcast *Things Mom Never Said: Secrets to Aging Well.*

She spent many years working in the local foods, design, and wellness industries, touting the importance of connected well-being, mindful eating, healthy advantages of sustainable design, and how it's possible to prevent and repair the effects aging. It wasn't until she found herself a victim of stress-related illness, that she knew she too had to become a healthier version of herself.

After experiencing manic depression and complete burnout, she charted her own personal path to wellness and her need to inspire other women grew. *Gen-X, the Adult Era: Designing a Life of Wellness* was born out of her personal experience and a lifelong passion for health, wellness, real food, design, and sustainability. April is now a health advocate, guiding others to stand up for their own health and well-being; a health educator providing science-based coaching; a podcast host exploring how each generation of women can live better; a wellness consultant supporting healthy lives through the built environment; and a positive inspiration in how finding balance is key to a healthy and happy life.

She created Wellness Design Group to show how blending the power of nature with the science of health and well-being helps you create a home that supports the inhabitants' health, honors their story, and respects the planet. Her degree in interior design and extensive education in construction technology sets her apart in the health and wellness industry. As a seasoned guide in the art of mindful living through design, she has a profound understanding of the impact of surroundings on well-being. April seamlessly integrates principles of wellness into the design process to ensure each space is not just visually stunning but also promotes a harmonious balance between aesthetics and well-being.

She knows that you can design the life you want—and the world you love. It is her mission to make the world a place where healthy and happy are the norm, not the exception.

The Shiz

/SHiz/
noun

1. stuff or something cool.
Ex. "This stuff is the shiz."

(citations)

1. Twisted Sister. 1984. "We're Not Gonna Take It." Stay Hungry. Atlantic Records
2. Waylon Jennings. 1980. "The Dukes of Hazard Theme." (Good Ol' Boys). Music Man. Sony Music
3. Gloria Loring. 1979 "The Facts of Life Theme." 100 Greatest TV Themes, Vol. 3. Universal Music Group
4. The reality of menopausal weight gain. Mayo Clinic Healthy Lifestyle: Women's Health Blog. https://www.mayoclinic.org/healthy-lifestyle/womens-health/in-depth/menopause-weight-gain/art-20046058. Accessed July 08, 2023
5. Bill Murray. (1981) *"John Winger."* Stripes. Universal Pictures
6. Brian O'Halloran. (1994) *"Dante Hicks."* Clerks. Miramax Films
7. America Ferrera. (2023) *"Gloria."* Barbie. Warner Bros
8. Eurythmics. 1985. "Sisters Are Doin' It For Themselves." Be Yourself Tonight. RCA Records
9. David Gerrold (1973) The Man Who Folded Himself. Random House
10. Billy Ocean. 1986. "When the Going Gets Tough, the Tough Get Going." Love Really Hurts Without You: The Greatest Hits of Billy Ocean. Sony Music Entertainment
11. Faith No More. (1989) "Epic." The Real Thing. Slash Records.
12. Tom Hanks. (1994) *"Forrest Gump."* Forrest Gump. Paramount Pictures
13. Beastie Boys. (1986) "[You Gotta] Fight For Your Right (To Party!)" Licensed to Ill. Def Jam Recordings
14. Becky Hensley (2021) "Breathe." Talking to the Wild.
15. Plato. (402a = DK22A6) Cratylus.
16. Sean Penn. (1982) *"Jeff Spicoli."* Fast Times at Ridgemont High. Universal Pictures
17. Winona Ryder. (1988) *"Veronica Sawyer."* Heathers. New World Pictures
18. The Rembrandts. (1995) "I'll Be There For You." L.P.. East West Records
19. Robert Downey Jr. (1987) *"Jack Jericho."* The Pick Up Artist. 20th Century

FOX

20. Eddy Murphy. Dan Aykroyd. (1983) *"Billy Ray Valentine & Louis Winthorpe III."* Trading Places. Paramount Pictures

21. En Vogue. (1992) "Free Your Mind." Funky Divas. Elektra Records

22. W. Sears, MD, M. Sears, RN (2010) *Prime Time Health: A Scientifically Proven Plan for Feeling Young and Living Longer.* Little Brown Spark

23. Billy Crystal. (1987) *"Miracle Max."* The Princess Bride. 20th Century FOX

24. Crispin Glover. (1985) *"George McFly."* Back to the Future. Universal Pictures

25. Janice Trachtman (2016) *Catching What Life Throws at You: Inspiring True Stories of Healing.* Janice Trachtman

26. Theo Tsaousides Ph.D. (2023) *What It Means to Be Truly Authentic.* Psychology Today. https://www.psychologytoday.com/us/blog/smashing-the-brainblocks/202211/what-it-means-to-be-truly-authentic

27. Brené Brown (2010) *The Gifts of Imperfection: Let Go of Who You Think You're Supposed to Be and Embrace Who You Are.* Hazelden

28. Molly Ringwald. (1985) *"Andie Walsh."* Pretty in Pink. Paramount Pictures

29. Emilio Estevez. (1985) *"Andrew Clark."* The Breakfast Club. Universal Pictures

30. Patrick Swayze. (1987) *"Johnny Castle."* Dirty Dancing. Artisan Entertainment

31. Eckhart Tolle. (1997) *The Power of Now A Guide to Spiritual Enlightenment.* New World Library (See also *(2019) What Is Self? Timeless Wisdom From The Archives.* https://www.youtube.com/watch?v=fPs510TWiOw)

32. Survivor. (1982) "Eye of the Tiger." Eye of the Tiger. Scotti Bros. Records

33. Frank Oz. (1980) *"Yoda."* The Empire Strikes Back. 20th Century FOX

34. Anthony Michael Hall. (1985) *"Brian Johnson."* The Breakfast Club. Universal Pictures

35. Melody Beattie. (1990) *The Language of Letting Go: Hazelden Meditation Series.* Hazelden Publishing

36. Eckhart Tolle. (2005) *A New Earth: Awakening to Your Life's Purpose.* Gratitude Chapter. Dutton/Penguin Group

37. Eckhart Tolle. (2005) *A New Earth: Awakening to Your Life's Purpose.* Gratitude Chapter. Dutton/Penguin Group

38. Robin Williams. (1989) *"Professor John Keating."* Dead Poets Society. Touchstone Pictures